Not to be Denied

The Whistling Girls & Crowing Hens Series
Book 1

Jan Anthony

Not to be Denied is a creative work of historical stories. Names, characters, places and incidents are products of the author's imagination and media articles and are used fictitiously and are not to be construed as real. Any resemblances to actual events, locales, organizations or persons, living or dead, are coincidental.

Copyright © by Jan Anthony 2024

No part of this book is to be reproduced, transmitted in any form or means; electronic or mechanical, stored in a retrieval system, photocopied, recorded, scanned, or otherwise copied. Any of these actions require the written permission of the author.

ISBN: 979-8-8691-4323-5

Library of Congress Preassigned Control Number: 2024902322

Not To Be Denied

The Whistling Girls & Crowing Hens Series
Book 1

Jan Anthony

*A creative memoir based on Bea Lindberg's
and Jan Anthony's letters,
prose, poetry, journals, diaries and imagination*

Mother Courage Press
Editor and Publisher, Jeanne Arnold

First Edition
With a few Author Changes

The Whistling Girls & Crowing Hens Series

Two straight married women risk families and careers, leave society's compulsory heterosexuality in 1972, and boldly thrive in an unchartered, intimate relationship. Jan and Bea experience historic events in the women's movement and gay/lesbian world in their 39 years together. Each book presents deeper levels on major topics and adventures.

The stand-alone books in this Whistling Girls & Crowing Hens Series will appeal to:

- young adults to appreciate what has come before them,
- elders to remember and respond to what they've survived,
- all readers to experience straight and lesbian lives, and
- women-loving-women who may have defied society's rules.

DEDICATION

Dedicated to the women in my life,
and all those who love them –
especially Bea for her love and her poems and journals. And to
those who love our stories.

PROLOGUE

Jan writes in her daily journal on January 1, 2017

My life has waited for my story! I can't believe the richness of what I've found in my files. I started compiling and writing in 1994: words expressing joy, love, gratitude, hurt, anger, and rejection, hundreds of poems, letters, journals, clippings and memories. I'll do my best to relate what happened in the depths, the turbulence, the heartbeats.

I think of Adrienne Rich's "Transcendental Etude" as her words rise from her book, *Dream of a Common Language*, challenging a braver me to proceed with my

"bits of yarn, calico and velvet scraps..."

I'd been

"... laying them out absently on the scrubbed board in the lamplight, with small rainbow-colored shells sent in cotton-wool from somewhere far away..."

In my retirement years, I picked up where I left off and began to write and edit more boldly, confident with

"... experienced fingers quietly pushing dark against bright, silk against roughness, pulling the tenets of a life together."

I will persevere,

"... practicing till strength and accuracy become one with the daring to leap into transcendence..."

For years my motto has been, "This or something better is now manifesting for me in totally harmonious and satisfying ways for the highest good of all concerned."

Many of these stories are real; some are speculation or fiction.

Some names have been changed; most are real people.

Let it begin.

CHAPTER ONE

Jan wrote on May 1, 1974

What were Bea and I thinking? Will we burn out and then life will go back to where it was before we surrendered to each other? Do we imagine that we can carry on indefinitely and keep our husbands and children at the same time? Will this be only a blip in our lives, a romantic memory to look back on as we move toward the future with our husbands and families in customary lives leading toward death? With few guidelines to help us, perhaps we can sustain our lover, husband, family and career.

Jan on September 10, 1971

Who could ask for anything more? Yet, in recent years, my life has not been as happy as I'd hoped and perhaps keeping a journal will help me sort out what's wrong with me.

The *Bay View News* editors asked me to work part-time starting tomorrow and I'll keep track of my thoughts and events during this significant personal and family adjustment.

My husband, Alex Carnigian, isn't happy about my working, but it's time for me to resume my professional life, especially after he demanded last year that I reject the career opportunity offered to me at the prestigious Winslow Foundation. What an opportunity that would have been. What a wimp I was to let him talk me out of it. Matt and Jenny are in school now, and our home overlooking Lake Michigan is totally remodeled, yet Alex makes me feel guilty for even considering my returning to a career.

I let that thrust me into a summer of deep loneliness, constantly playing *Sgt. Pepper's Lonely Hearts Club Band* and being "Eleanor Rigby." I wrote poetry that no one read and talked to myself with no one listening.

While studying books like William Braden's *The Private Sea, LSD & the Search for God*, a William James quote inspired me. "Does God really exist? How does he exist? What is he? Are they irrelevant questions? Not God, but life, more life, a larger, more satisfying life, is in the last analysis the end of religion. The love of life at any and every level of development is the religious impulse."

I dreamed of becoming a certified Unitarian Universalist religious educator and in October 1967, I began with a class at UW-Milwaukee on the philosophy of the world's religious leaders. We started with fathers, kings and shamans, heroes and saints, saviors and teachers, even Ayn Rand. But Alex also squelched that career illusion.

Yet who am I to have such lofty ambitions—to be a professional in a compassionate spiritual setting? Even as a volunteer, I've been sucked into intense, uncompassionate conflicts with individuals in separate situations where I had to choose between my integrity and convictions or that of the organization. I chose to do what I thought was right for each organization—as if each would not survive without my being involved in saving it.

While reading William Faulkner's *Light in August* one sunny morning, sitting upright in bed after the kids went to school, I paused to contemplate his main character, Joe Christmas. Even with the character's shockingly raunchy racist and sexual behavior, I could identify with his agonizing vulnerability. I looked across the bright bedroom and saw my full self in the vanity mirror. Faulkner's book rested on my bent knees, covered with my red and gold bedspread. White pillows billowed behind me. Lake Michigan and the morning light glowed through the window to the mirror.

"Joe Christmas," I thought as if communicating with the image in front of me. "Joe Christmas. JC. Jesus Christ. Jesus Christ!" That revelation leapt to "JC. Jan Carnigian!" I never thought of my initials as JC. I shuddered and shook that image out of my soul like a Faulkner's Mississippi mongrel hound would shake swampy river water off her boney body.

Two weeks ago, the managing editor of our local daily newspaper called me to ask if I'd work there part-time. They needed an all-purpose, part-time reporter. By now, my husband had run out of excuses to stop me; Jenny was in third grade and Matt was in fifth. My children could manage an hour in the afternoon until I came home from work. With my mother institutionalized for so many years, I pretty much took care of myself since I was ten.

When I went to interview for the job, the editor greeted me like a long-lost niece and started selling the job to me. Then he took me into the managing editor, who remembered me from teaching his university journalism class, and that rascal turned into a Dutch uncle. He was so solicitous I couldn't believe it. He made a reference to my mind being like a "steel trap" and that I'd learn the mechanics of the job quickly. I kept my perspective, thinking that after all this time of being a homemaker, my mind was more like a mousetrap and a rusty one at that.

They want me anyway and on my terms—so far. I'll be working on Tuesdays and Thursdays, plus filling in when a reporter is ill, pregnant, or drying out in an alcoholic treatment center.

Alex told me again that he's always been against the concept of working mothers. I said that I'd be a mother who worked and stressed a reassuring approach that all would go well and avoided the head-on confrontations with him that I'd failed to win in the past.

My one annual respite from being a homemaker and wife that he accepts is my legacy of decorating floats for two or three weeks before the 4th of July. Alex always helps my dad and me with this tradition after he leaves his job for the day. His sister, Var, and niece, Sona, take care of Matt and Jenny. It's truly a family tradition for me, a proud heritage. Even when I was six- months pregnant with Jenny, I climbed tall, wobbly ladders and twisted myself into strange positions to decorate those floats.

My volunteer work publicizing my two community programs has paid off because I kept myself visible and appreciated, but having projects unrelated to being a wife, mother and domestic worker are ignored or merely tolerated at home and I've avoided daily personal journaling, except for the poem that I wrote for Alex's Valentine.

Frustration

Over twenty years together
and a million mundane matters
can leave a legacy of broken fragments
of old truth.
With romantic dreams
obscured by realities of life
we need not mourn the superficial lost love
of our youth.

Oh, the word is still important,
 yet it cannot stand alone,
spoken in an empty room, it echoes
emptiness.

To turn to separate interests
need not mean "turn away."
Our knowledge and experience can make
our lives profound.
As separate selves together,
rather than subordinates,
we can complete our meanings and stress
our common ground.

Oh, the word is still important,
yet it cannot stand alone,
spoken in an empty room, it echoes
hollowness.

We must not value first
what we desire in each other.
We must allow each other to live free,
without pretensions.
Then real oneness replaces tolerance;
a knowing joy replaces dreams.
Shattered hearts from things not shared are
reconciled by new dimensions.

Oh, the word is still important,
yet it cannot stand alone,
spoken in a lonely room, it echoes
loneliness.

The only other creations I've accomplished recently were to reupholster a four-piece sectional sofa and sew a hundred yards of fabric into draperies for our home.

But! I must not omit my most important creative work: my Unitarian Universalist Sunday school, my UU friends like Marge Manley, Anna Spence, Bea Lindberg and other dedicated volunteer teachers.

Bea Lindberg and I collaborated on the biography course she compiled about people who made a difference. She chose adventurers Oliver Perry, Richard Byrd, Ernest Shackleton, Thor Heyerdahl and Sir Francis Chichester who, at 72, was the first person to sail singlehandedly around the world on the Gypsy Moth IV.

I looked at her proposed curriculum—all men, all single-minded, inflexible, overwhelming egotists. No wonder they reached their goals—or died doing it. What about women? What about improving society? Women are resolute too. I added Dr. Elizabeth Blackwell, Jane Addams, Clara Barton and Maria Montessori, a noteworthy person to me because I helped develop our first Montessori school so my pre-schoolers, Matt and Jenny and others could benefit from Montessori's methods.

So Bea and I became team teachers and on my Sundays, I hoped to inspire my class about women and their accomplishments. I'm sure her classes with her bold male adventurers and her lucid story-telling talents were much more exciting than mine.

With taking on my reporting job at the newspaper, I'll cut back from church school responsibilities, but I'll be there if that team needs me—because I need them.

It's time. I'm eager, even if I'm not completely prepared. I can't get into too much trouble—I hope.

Jan on September 12, 1971

I earned a by-line on the first story of my first day! I was to gather women's opinions on TV sports that aired all weekend. Only two months ago, the team with Neil Armstrong, Buzz Aldrin and Michael Young deserved our foremost attention. Now baseball is at the peak of action with Ernie Banks and Ron Santo earning cheers with the World Series coming up and football is already here with quarterbacks to watch like Bart Starr and O.J. Simpson.

"Let's see what you can come up with for a story," dared my editor.

To get started, I called Adele McEwen, my friend and neighbor with a droll sense of humor and she gladly told me her opinion plus another woman's name to call. I'm happy I'd gone to our area's first NOW organizational meeting last month. Some of the members gave me colorful comments saying, for example, "Leave your husbands to the stultifying atmosphere of cigar smoke and beer" or "Why fight it and join the crowd."

Dramatically, my feature covered the top half of the page, including an action football photo and I heard my co-workers laugh while reading the story when the fresh-off-the-press newspaper was dropped on each of their desks that afternoon.

Of course, I was pleased and proud of myself, but when I came home, the meatloaf for supper was more important to the family than my successful feature in this afternoon's paper.

I'm lucky I've made good connections with newspaper people. It may have been destiny to spend each Saturday night during my high school years with Marty and Susan, daughters of Carol and Don MacFarland. Don was the publisher of our local paper and I credit him as my career coach who encouraged me to go to college. He even offered me financial support if I needed it. That motivated me to give college a try even though my father had medical bills for my mother and made little money being a sign painter in our little city.

I didn't need to ask the MacFarlands for money. I went to the University of Wisconsin's Oshkosh Extension for two years and lived at home before going to the Madison campus. That saved money and I made new friends, including some faculty members.

After getting married between semesters of my college senior year and teaching high school English and journalism in two small Wisconsin towns, my second lieutenant husband and I lived near Fort Monmouth in New Jersey until I became an Army dependent waiting in Lakeshore Bay for my overseas port call to join him in Frankfurt, Germany. I'd loved to have found a room in New York City and worked as a waitress, but I returned home and worked in a factory spraying armature disks. I didn't tell my employer that I was a teacher; they never would have hired me. Nor did I tell them I was going to be there for only a couple of months. Big deal. It took only two minutes to train me.

While waiting, I chose to sleep in a rooming house rather than stay with my father and his live-in woman friend or with my in-law family with three generations squeezed into their tiny house. My room was grim but clean. The mattress suffered from sagging springs and it had two basketball-sized holes that I avoided by curling myself around them. I never complained about the mattress. I played my 78-rpm phonograph records in my room and spent hours typing my personal history and letters and no one complained about that.

When Don MacFarland found out I was back in town, he invited me to stay with their daughters while they went on an extended vacation. They trusted me with their two daughters, their pets, their beautiful home and their expensive cars. When they returned and I still had no port call, he hired me as a librarian helper for the paper's morgue. When I finally left for Germany three months later, Don MacFarland wrote an open letter recommending me for any job I applied for; he would vouch for my claim that I could do whatever it was that I said I could do.

His letter was an affirmation that has always given me the courage and strength to achieve what I wanted or needed to accomplish.

Because of so many veterans entering college on the G.I. Bill, the normally mandatory courses in math and foreign language were dropped. That eliminated classes that probably would be impossible for me to pass.

With great surprise and gratitude, I graduated in June 1953 from the University of Wisconsin in Madison with academic honors.

Jan on September 16, 1971

If the two-year University of Wisconsin Extension program had not been developed across the state to provide college opportunities for veterans using the G.I. Bill, I probably would not have gone on to school. My mentors had motivated me and my dad told me to give it a try. Tuition was $65 a semester and when the bills piled up for Mom's care at Winnebago, he kept telling its ominous bill collector that he had only one option to pay and that was for my education—"For the future of the Country," he claimed. I was 17 when I graduated from Roosevelt High and thought I couldn't get a proper job until I was at least 18. I wonder what that "proper job" might have been? Also, I could live at home and help my dad.

Alex pushed skids of Midwestern Publishing books and games to the loading docks and saved money for college. One time he told me that he didn't think it was worth going on to college. His mother needed him to earn a salary to help her with her expenses. I told him that I wouldn't expect to be with someone who wasn't as well educated as I was. That changed his mind, but he would have gone on to school sometime. He was too intelligent not to go even though his mother could have used financial support after he turned 18 and lost her Aid For Dependent Children benefits. He didn't leave her destitute, however, because his married sister, Var, her husband, John, and their newborn daughter, Sona, would fill the tiny house.

I loved Alex for the saneness, safety and security and for his goodness and love of me. He was handsome too. And kind and gentle.

We'd play tennis together and we'd watch each other play on several city league baseball and basketball teams. I was recruited and played boring baseball in order to play basketball with a city team that awarded me with a slippery green satin basketball jacket with an easy opening zipper that was handy to wear when we were intimate—but just necking. We both did well in that game together. One summer, on our living room couch with our clothes on, we accidentally discovered, much to my surprise and satisfaction the passionate greatness of my first orgasm. We did not want to get pregnant. We wanted to finish college. Abortion was not an option. I never asked about condoms. Ironically, it took over five years after we married to get pregnant with our first child.

By entering the UW-Extension program, I found myself entering a new school on my own. Most of my girlfriends got jobs or married their high school sweethearts and got pregnant. I excelled in extra-curricular activities. I was needed at the Varsity View newspaper. While singing and acting at various talent and dramatic events, I found a calling for myself in promoting the events. No school athletic teams nor gym classes were required, but the men's tennis team needed another player for a tournament and I became the first woman to play with a men's UW team sport in an intercollegiate event.

The *Bay View News* sports page read, "For the first time in history, a girl will take part in the Wisconsin Extension Conference Men's Athletic Event. She is Jan Anthony from the Oshkosh Extension. She will compete in the all-extension Tennis Tournament in Madison." I tried but couldn't keep up with the guys. I lost in the first round when the nervous male lobbed every ball behind me and completely threw off my game. What a cheap shot.

Alex on March 20-24, 1949

Jan Anthony

You said to write it, here it goes. We have fun together. When we kiss, there is no pressure or meaning barred. You agree that far. I take care of the pressure when I put my bear hug on you, but the meaning comes from both parties, I find myself getting hugged back with meaning, too.

You say you've got to feel it all the time, not only during the night and the day after. All week for me. I told you I love you. The last time I said that was on October 25, 1947. Remember? You laughed that time. That hurt something terrific, worse than my football injury that night. This time you didn't laugh, did you?

Funny—a guy loving his best friend.

Here is my interpretation. Love is when you look forward and backward—forward to being with her and doing things, backward to things done and undone, good and bad and still have fun. You gotta like things in common, OK? Let's delve: We like athletics except for baseball. Both of us. That's a lot of time taken up right there. I like to be with you. I think you said that for you too! We find things to talk about. Some are not pleasant but we find ourselves earnestly discussing them, not arguing—discussing.

Now then, you like to laugh and have fun at parties. I do too, but I have my fun observing the people having fun, but here's the catch. Definition of conditioned reflex, associating pleasant symbols to mannerisms. Pleasant symbols—Jan Anthony and food—you first. Just think. I could condition myself to have fun.

You like to go to jazz places: the Blue Note and Stage Door. You know that I don't. You like to see bands and stuff too. The thing is, I don't enjoy jitterbugging like you do. But I could learn to like it. What's no false front? Formal dances—the only thing against them is no ping pong. Once when you asked me to do one, I was broke, no dough. But now I can go, Jan, if you let me take you.

I told you I was afraid of you. I can't act naturally in front of you. It's only something inside. I joke around with the best of them. You never see it though. Any other girl is easy, but I could if things were the way we were thinking Saturday. Your heart was beating terrifically fast. I could feel it through your hands, almost any place I had my arms. Don't worry. Mine was too, like a trip hammer. What do we need, a blueprint?

You said, "What could it hurt if we just let things happen." You said it might start and end. It can't end without some sound reason. Trifles are worked out. We're good at working things out, right? If it did end, it would have to be somebody's fault. It wouldn't just happen. Play the percentages, like ping pong. If you hot spike like mad, you won't hit on all of them but enough to win. If your defense is hot, be defensive. You won't return them all but you can win by letting the other side jag up. If you win fine, if you lose, it doesn't hurt. It's only a game. Of course, our discourse has different losses, but Ah nuts—it can be worked out—COMPROMISE—both give in to a common cause. You like to laugh and be gay, but when you're with me, you accept a different attitude. You don't act as you do otherwise and we still have fun. You've been compromising for three years and didn't realize it.

You base your conclusion on my action at parties from two things. I said eight words all night at one party and your own party last year. We've never gone to a party together yet this year. I've been to several and I can't recollect being glum or silent-Alex yet—You haven't seen this guy in action yet.

I thought I knew you but I'll never figure you out. The one I know now is different. You take things seriously and think instead of discarding them—right? 17-chronologically; mentally? You must be different. Look how you acted Saturday. You didn't know what to say. You said, "We're so different." At the same time, I find myself being pulled close and hugged and kissed.

Do you follow me in that two people who are carefree and gay eventually go to pot, but if one sees reality, the two work like a machine with a regulator? Our regulator could be my sense of reality. Can't overdo gaiety because I could tell you about it. You, in turn, could keep me from being a dud and you truthfully can, Jan.

> Brush the sleep from your eyes
> And try to realize
> That the ache in my heart is for you.
> Original, what?
> What are we going to do?
> Let it ride from week to week, month to month.

If you could ever say I love you to me, I think I'd be a different guy, ever so happy, and wonderfully content. I felt wonderfully content the last two weeks. I ask if I'm overdoing things. You say no. Would you say no to any guy who kissed you like that?

All I ask is a chance, Jan. If I flop, then it's my fault. No harm in trying, is there? As you read this, I will be watching you—standing or sitting next to you. I hope you can follow my terrible grammar and punctuation. As you read, you questioned some things, but you've already asked them. Sooo—It's your move, Jan.

Love, Alex

Jan on September 21, 1971

I compromised. And in our high school senior year, we've become a couple ever since. I needed someone stable and that's what he is—and kind. Besides, I had three sophomore girls hanging around and one, I knew, had a serious crush on me.

   Back in ninth grade, innocent pajama parties packed girls together in various homes. I don't recall what house I was at for this PJ party, but I do remember what happened. Three or four of us lay crossways on a day bed set up in the living room. A new girl I hardly knew was stretched out next to me on my left. Our space was dark except for the slice of light from a slightly opened door. Light or dark, a lot of giggling rippled throughout the house. Tolerant chaperoning parents tried to sleep as far away as possible from the noisy nonsense.
   The tension between the two of us grew as we whispered together and as others quieted down. For fun, we kissed each other good night. Perhaps it was her first kiss but it touched our longing inner selves and we continued, lying next to each other in our pajamas, holding each other close for hours until the door opened wider as someone entered the room and we bolted to change our positions.
   What was happening to me, to us? I didn't even know her and I certainly didn't understand what was going on inside of me. After breakfast, we left to go our separate ways, but on Monday she was waiting for me outside after school.
   My best friend Nazaly was aware of her presence but oblivious of the peculiar feelings between us. This girl had a crush on me! She became obsessed, followed me around, and scared me. I didn't understand nor did I like her dependency and the way she looked at me in front of others. I had no one to talk with about my turbulent feelings. All the movies had girls being mushy for boys. All the lyrics on The Hit Parade sang about girls and boys, women and men. What was I feeling? What was I? When Naz asked me what made me so moody so suddenly and for so long. I couldn't tell her because I knew what I was experiencing was wrong. I'd changed, becoming distracted, isolated, moody, secretive, and alone. Nazaly couldn't understand what I was going through and I couldn't tell

her. And I think I stopped practice-kissing girls after that—for a while anyway.

The new girl never became closer to me as a friend or—whatever. Her father worked for the government and her family was transferred to Washington, D.C. She sent me a letter that I lost, but I did find a snapshot of her wearing a double-buttoned dark jacket standing in front of a hotel lobby door. A note on the back said, "Me at the R. Hotel. February 1, 1946."

Sometime later, a rumor went around that she committed suicide.

When Alex wasn't playing ping pong in the rec room at a party, putting a shot at a track meet or jagging about with his friends, Alex always seemed to be hanging around behind me and my friends, except during our high school junior year when he dated a gal named Fay.

Jan on September 30, 1971

We were Mutt and Jeff, my friend Nazaly and I, she reaching the five-foot mark and weighing about 100 pounds, and I at five-feet-seven inches tall and 135 pounds. My Armenian friend never went out with boys and was the exact opposite of me in many ways. Our opposites attracted and we respected each other's attributes. Sometimes she'd frustrate me because she wouldn't go to plays or athletic events with me in Milwaukee or Chicago. She was obedient; I was independent. She was loyal and conscientious. Nazaly was six of one; I was half-a-dozen of the other. In spite of my somewhat weird personality, she stuck with me. She was always there to help and back me up. It was a great feeling to have a true friend. She was a better friend to me than I was to her.

During school day mornings, the phone would jar me out of bed with the cheerful yet resigned voice of my loyal Nazaly with her wake-up call. I'd jump into some clothes, comb out my pin curls, run out the back door and down the alley where she'd be standing next to the light pole right in the center of my alley view, waiting patiently in her dark blue floral babushka wrapped around her head, her Navy pea coat, most often a plaid, pleated skirt, rumpled bobby sox and saddle shoes. We'd walk to school or catch a ride whenever possible from someone else's dad.

This June seemed tragic because Gloria and Billie and ten of our best friends graduated, leaving Naz and me looking forward in despair without our senior friends for our remaining Roosevelt High years. The two of us were compensated somewhat when we were invited to Gloria's house for their graduation slumber party. Another of their classmates, a girl I'd never noticed before, was invited too, and I liked her laugh when she responded to my goofy behavior during that night.

Karen and I would soon become more than the best of friends. Karen took me away from one kind of madness and set me on another that was much more fun. Karen bought me into her home, where her mother nurtured me with her charming accent and sweet smile. I made them laugh, too, and helped them with the two little offspring from Karen's mother's second marriage.

Most of Nazaly's and my senior friends went off to work or were married after they graduated. Only Gloria Stevens and Donna Durand went on and enrolled as Lakeshore's School of Nursing students, moved to the dorm, and lived and worked there under constant supervision and discipline to protect any of the students from "going astray" in this perilous world.

Society's controls were absolute. The fear of pregnancy, being ostracized as a loose or fallen woman, and having to get married kept many a girl from getting that way.

Rather than look for a job, Karen stayed home while her mother went to France to visit her parents. Karen's firefighter father was away most of the time.

Nazaly got my leftover time. What kind of a friend was I, leaving her high and dry, almost abandoning her? She didn't know, nor did anyone else, about our relationship, especially Alex who found a different girlfriend from the other side of town at the same time I found Karen.

I practically lived at Karen's house. The boys in Karen's neighborhood hovered and often landed on her porch for 500 Rummy and a party or two until they got drunk and threw up. We cleaned up before Karen's dad came home in the morning. But we found each other's company much more satisfying. One night on her porch, when she put her hands on each side of my face, drew me near her, and kissed me goodnight, I prolonged this kiss and pressed my body into hers. I'd finally found the joyful thrill of a full-blown infatuation and a passionate curiosity that allowed me to find love and joy in an intense experience that electrified my summer of '47" and all of my junior year in high school.

I'd spring off the porch and onto my bike and I sailed from her side of town to mine; my hands hardly touched the handlebars with my arms stretched out toward the sky. We sustained and expanded our secret feelings with a fun-loving, sensitive, laugh-filled, kissing, hugging, sleeping-together primary relationship.

She was conceited, stubborn, and proud, and I would do anything in the world for her. Karen knew much more than I and I grew more mature trying to catch up with her. Before I knew her, I was an easy mark to make friends, ready to do almost anything for the asking. I played the part of a fool because I didn't want to be abandoned. I'd been hurt when fair-weather friends let me down. She taught me to take care of myself first, then the other person. This may be a crude philosophy, but I've saved myself from heartaches and disappointments, and I can still help others.

Though two years older than I, she chose me over male dates as her significant person. She was my Lauren Bacall; she called me "Steve" and I called her "Slim" as in *To Have and Have Not*.

I chose her to be my chaperone at a Milwaukee daily newspaper's tennis tournament and we stayed downtown at the Wisconsin Hotel. What a chaperone! She arranged for one of her boyfriends to bring another guy and we drove about town and partied. Again, I didn't get past the first round, but this time I had an excuse for exhaustion beyond my self-taught tennis technique.

Each night when I was at home, I'd sit cross-legged on my lower bunk bed, play solitaire, and listen to Chicago's WMAQ disk jockey Dave Garroway talk about jazz and The Blue Note Jazz Club. He'd play music until after 1:00 a.m. He was my mentor now, playing cool records of Sarah Vaughn, Ella Fitzgerald, and loud Stan Kenton with June Christie, Woody Herman with trombonist Bill Harris—all that jazz. For live music, I'd take the bus to Milwaukee and go to the Eagles Club to stand against the stage and let the music pound through me. Knowing how much I loved her voice, my dad actually took me to Chicago to see Sarah Vaughn at The Blue Note.

I worked for several months in the record department at Green's Music Store. Jazz players always hung out there and Nat Green's band was the best local band for us to jitterbug to their music. But Ken Griffin's organ music and "You Can't Be True Dear" was the best seller at the store.

What a joy it was to see Karen walk into the store on Friday night to spend time with me after work. She must have arranged for a babysitter for her little brother and baby sister.

We slept together as often as possible, either in her parents' bed when her father was away or in her narrow bed in the second bedroom with her brother and sister sleeping across from us. We were always quite reserved in our holding each other close; we never fondled each other in intimate places.

She knew little about human sexuality and I knew even less. If you wore yellow on Thursdays, or was it green, you were a fairy, queer or fag. We didn't want any of that. I didn't even know the words "lesbian" and "homosexual" at the time. But we knew enough to keep our love hidden. Karen and I double-dated at times, with her in the back seat of the car and me in the front. Once my date told her date that I was a prick teaser and he didn't want to go out with me until I "put-out," but how could I be that when I've never touched one? No loss for me anyhow.

Karen's mother's presence diminished our time together at their house, and we both had to get on with life: her factory job and my Roosevelt High activities, but that didn't mean that Karen couldn't come to my house and stay overnight. Late one night, I heard a knock at my side door. It was Karen. She had escaped from almost being raped at Beach Point's golf course parking lot with the lighthouse on the north and the view of Lakeshore Bay's reflected lights on the lake to the south. The law would patrol regularly and flash beams of lights through the steamy windows, break up couples and send them home. This time Karen didn't wait, couldn't wait and walked the four miles to my house. Every time a car came by, she'd stoop in the gutter or behind a bush or tree so she wouldn't be caught on the road. Once Karen had a rowdy fight with her mother and asked my dad if she could stay with me. He approved and I relished taking care of her and sleeping with her in my upper bunk for a week before she returned home.

This undated letter came a few days after Karen returned home.

Dear Jan,

I want to thank you for everything you did for me this week. You were swell. I'm sorry about last night. I know I shouldn't have sworn at you but you know as well as I that I didn't mean it.

Well, I guess that's all—It's been nice knowing you. We always had good times together & will have a lot to remember. Good & Bad—

I guess you think I'm a rat—I guess we weren't meant for each other. I'm not meant for anyone—

Love,
Karen

On that night, we finally broke up. Carol was with us for a pajama party at my house when my dad was away. She was amazed at the intensity of our quarrel as we divided our co-mingled record collection. We almost threw records at each other while our friend sat in the corner wondering what was going on and why the terrible rage. The records that we both danced to and loved ended in two stacks: hers and hers.

It was time. I was 16 and still in school. We returned to our separate lives. What were the alternatives? I heard later that she married, gave birth to a son and named him Steve.

On the rainy night of October 27, 1947, my dad got a phone call from the sheriff in response to a call from a person living on Wood Lane. The caller said that a woman was shouting and pacing up and down this dead-end gravel road with a black and white dog on a leash. They drove to investigate and found my hysterical mother, lost and looking for her cousin's house. They couldn't find the dog. They put Mother in the car and would pick up my dad to be with her at the sheriff's station.

I was frantic when my dad hung up the phone and told me what they had said. I immediately grabbed my jacket and a flashlight and ran out to find Lady; perhaps her leash was caught on something or she ran away when the sheriff's car came, or she was injured—or run over. I ran west toward Roosevelt on streets I knew so well but there were fields of corn across from Roosevelt, and Wood Lane was only a lane of shabby houses that I'd never been near, west of the standing stalks of corn scratching against each other in the

October wind. I yelled and screamed for Lady for hours. I knew I had lost Lady —and my mother again.

Looking for comfort, I walked another mile south to Karen's house where they took me in, dried me off, gave me something warm to drink, and called my dad who wasn't there. I waited with them until he was and then Karen's father drove me home. Lady had found her own way home without me. Not all was lost. I didn't lose my Lady.

The next day, my mother was taken to St. Mary's Hill in Milwaukee. The nuns, wearing their black and white garments, carried enamel trays and pitchers up and down Gothic hallways as they had done for centuries of caring for the infirm and insane.

I'd go alone to see plays at the Davidson Theater in Milwaukee across the square from the end of the bus line. I'd purchased a first-row balcony center ticket for *The Streetcar Named Desire* with Uta Hagen and Anthony Quinn. I'd be an actor someday soon and Tennessee William was my hero, even though I may have missed several nuances of the plot. I felt that I wasn't in the audience; I was living on the stage, in the script, surviving the conflicts of power and love, submission and sexuality. When "the kind gentleman" came to take Blanche away after her illusions were shattered and violence finally crushed her frail spirit, my soul became one with Blanche. Dead silence enveloped the audience when the curtain closed, and then the loud applause shocked me as if someone had slapped me in the face and back to reality—my reality.

Jan on October 3, 1971

My New Year's Eve in 1962 was a night to celebrate my family: my successful husband, smart young son and three-month-old, perfectly magnificent daughter. Our high school couple friends met at the Joan and Bob's, who decorated their basement with colorful furniture, a bar, and a smooth place to dance. I was bursting with happiness—plus a few drinks, when Joan played the new rage "The Twist" on the phonograph. Chubby Checker's rasping voice thumped rocking rhythms. We happy celebrators jumped in and danced with elbows out and hands flapping. Our toes spun while our legs gyrated our upper and lower torsos in opposite directions as I'd seen on TV with trendy young dancing couples twisting for joy.

I remembered how to dance the Charleston from a skit we did in college—and my teenage years when I led the girls as we jitterbugged wildly at our high school dances.

The Twist was a snap for me and I danced it with gusto. Alex wouldn't join us. The way he responded, you'd have thought I did "The Stripper." Was this the way for a mother, his wife, to act?! After he told me I was lewd, he sulked on the way home, paid Var and Sona for babysitting and drove them home. I went to bed.

The phone rang at 4 a.m. It was Var. The tavern next store caught on fire from a cigarette dropped in a booth cushion and their restaurant with its adjoining wall was ablaze too. From March 1960 to December 31, 1961, Var and Sona lost their mother and grandmother, their husband and father, their restaurant and their home.

We took them in to stay with us in our upstairs apartment and while they lived with us they picked through every ash of their charred belongings. Alex changed jobs and moved to initiate a new computer system that was to be set up at Midwestern Publishing less than a mile from our home. Between his job changes, we decided to drive to Florida and take a break from our cluttered and depressed houseguests and give them a chance to solve some of their issues on their own.

My dad offered us his Rambler station wagon. Matt could play in the flattened back area; he even had his little potty chair back there. Jenny, at three months, nursed all the way to Florida, where we stayed at an almost seedy but clean "El Retiro" kitchenette near St. Petersburg. Matt chased seagulls and collected shells. Alex collapsed in the sun.

When we returned from Florida, nothing had changed.

CHAPTER TWO

Jan on April 5, 1972

Abortion, suicide, adoption, marriage, parenting, teenage mothers, family planning and other medical, health and women's topics became many of my assignments as a part-time reporter at the *Bay View News*; and that attracted the attention of healthcare professionals, including Nick Dixon, a new Lakeshore Medical Center executive, a neighbor with a Unitarian family like ours.

One evening Nick strolled the half-block to the large home we moved to on South Main Street and offered me a part-time job as Lakeshore Med's small-scale public relations person to create a newsletter, take some photos and write some newspaper releases. His wife, Diana, recommended me to him. I looked at my husband who was pouring Nick a generous glass of homemade cherry wine and proposed to keep my contact with the newspaper and work part-time at the hospital. I couldn't miss this opportunity. Lakeshore Med was two blocks away and I'd do much of that work at home. Sooner or later, one of my employers could take me on full-time, but if they kept me working at less than half-time, they wouldn't have to pay any benefits. I didn't need benefits when my husband was so bountifully insured in his successful position. Also, I liked to turn down work assignments when I wanted to be with my family. That was my pleasant but inexpensive salary decision.

I told Nick that I'd start on June 9. I now have two part-time jobs, plus my Unitarian Universalist church, peace and ecology activities—and as always, helping my father build and decorate 4th of July parade floats.

"Before all else, you are a wife and mother," Alex pontificated. I am also a human being!

With my work commitments, I found new friends, new freedom and a broader appreciation of other professions. I was also learning again to love and respect myself. My energies for others and for my children were boundless. And as in the past, I met almost every need that my husband requested.

Jan on May 9, 1972

My capacity for love seems infinite; my hunger for it too. Being an only child made me aware of what it takes to please others—to replace the loss of loved ones.

Perhaps that's why it's fate for me to be in a profession that helps the caretaker, the hospital worker, the patient, and even the community. Compared to the stress of being a social worker, the disciplinary necessities of teaching, my rebellion from the restraints of the German Lutheran tradition, my finding the freedom of being a Unitarian and my need to communicate with others at a spiritually gratifying level make hospital public relations an authentic match for me.

All I have to do is report to my boss, keep everyone else happy and project in every way the hospital's positive image. It's a challenging, delightful and inspiring tightrope-walking job working with others in insignificant ways, with political and economic issues, and even occasionally in life and death situations.

I also have to keep in balance my joy of loving my family, my best friend Marge and our secret.

After a bit of orientation to my hospital job, I wanted to experience a Friday night in the emergency room. Following my regular Friday night folk dancing and party that I left at midnight, I entered the ER with a camera, ready at that fateful hour when the taverns close and the drunks hit the streets.

I hung around until 3 a.m. The only emergency incidents that night had to do with anal sphincters—and that was hardly photographic.

An old lady walked in, complaining of dark stools and some pain. She was asked if she had a private physician. Well, yes, but it was too late to call, she said. They called him and the physician grumbled test orders and granted permission for the emergency resident to take charge. A technologist was called in, the patient was placed on a cart and when the tech arrived at 2 a.m., he was given a sample of her stool to analyze in the lab. Perhaps her loneliness aggravated her minor complaint into a genuine attack. Maybe she needed a friend more than treatment. Relating those feelings to stool samples may oversimplify this woman's problem. I marveled at the patience the medical team maintained.

I wandered about the halls, talking with nurses, aides and night staff personnel while I waited for something big to break loose in the ER.

Drawn to a light at the end of the hall in the medical intensive care unit, I walked toward it to find out what was going on in the bright room beyond, passing quiet, dark rooms emitting only sleeping patients' sounds.

I looked through the open door and saw two green-robed nurses bathing a youth, preparing him for a meal, and keeping him alive with electric wire sensors and plastic tubes. The nurses responded to me with a smile as I stood outside the room watching.

The youth, who had been critically injured in a car crash, was moved on his side to be bathed, exercised and massaged. When he saw me at the door, he acknowledged my presence with staring concentration. Only his observing eyes moved; they did not signal understanding.

"He's really alert tonight," said one nurse.

"He's much better than he was," said the other. They scurried about the intensely lit room massaging his muscles, exercising his limbs and helping him to urinate. This Christ-like figure is a 13-year-old, blond, tall boy incapacitated by the unexpected events of a crash where his father was killed, his mother widowed with three other children and his future hanging on the hope that he'll respond to this nurturing environment.

They connected a tube of green food to a plastic hose through his nose and gently forced the nutrients through the tube and into his stomach. The green in the tube matched the green of the gowns covering the nurses' regular white uniforms.

The boy's eyes never left me watching from the door as I, watching in return, observed the sterile-robed women caring for this lamb of a child who was covered only around his loins so he could be easily moved and cleaned and fed and maybe feel the love they would convey to help him understand that somebody wanted him to struggle to live.

Irrational optimism kept these nurses nursing. I sensed that they would never give up.

I turned away and walked down the steps to the surgical intensive care unit, which seemed dark and calm except for the shaded lights of the nurses' station and the sudden sound of clatter and a splash jarring the silence.

An elderly man had reached for a water pitcher and knocked it over in the attempt.

All was quiet there again soon and I went back down to the ER.

"Nothing new, Jan. We'll have to have you come here every night. You're good luck."

Then the phone rang and a male aide picked up the receiver, listened intently, cupped his hand across the phone and repeated the incident to the nurse. "This gal was walking home with her boyfriend when he had pain and an uncontrollable urge to defecate. He did, next to the sidewalk and she's worried about him and doesn't know what to do."

The nurse raised her eyebrow, tilting her head to the side and said quietly from the corner of her mouth, "Tell her to get a new boyfriend—" and then quickly added, "Have her bring him in and we'll talk with him."

The resident physician had been awakened that night for two excrement problems. Yet they were human problems and they were responded to. Even the med-tech who was dragged out of his house twice on a wintry night was happy because he had two calls—that earned him double pay. He had managed to get home between calls, which gave him double credit for the fecal matter he had to analyze.

I walked through the shadowed, quiet halls once more that night. Only tiny rays of call lights from patient doors to the nursing station, only the swooshing sound of nurses' nylon hose brushing as they walked on their soft-soled shoes signaled activity on this night.

I went home at 3:30 a.m. feeling happy for a quiet night. I had missed the excitement of the intense impact of emergency room trauma, yet I gained insight into the real nightlife of the hospital. The knifing and the gunshot wounds would make the news, yet it's the shit work that people need to be done most often.

Twenty minutes after I left, the surgical intensive care nurse who had wiped up the spilled water and picked up the pitcher found her elderly patient dead. She remembered what he had said then, that she shouldn't bother replacing the water. He had had enough, he told her. After she found him, she covered his body and called the resident doctor who pronounced him dead. She and her aide put the body into a steel box with the cover level to the top of the gurney top, and draped it with a cloth. It looked like she was pushing an empty cart as she wheeled him down the hall, onto the elevator and down to the morgue, where his name on a tag tied to his toe would soon be read by a funeral director.

And upstairs on the fifth floor, twins were born to a young couple beginning their family and their claim to their own kind of immortality.

I asked Randy King, my office partner, to evaluate what I wrote about that night. Since then, we've exchanged feelings about life in intense and lengthy conversations with this administrative assistant. We agree on almost every political and religious topic. He finds me willing to share my experiences, be non-judgmental about his and to be somewhat wise, probably because I'm older and more liberal than most others my age.

I'll not risk all my life's details in exchange for his. I'm always guarded about my personal thoughts, but I'm open to listening to his perceptions, sensing ambivalence and confusion about lifestyle options as a post-graduate student. Randy and I spent many hours during his holiday breaks and summer months at work talking in our little, quiet hospital basement office.

He was stressed out by anti-Vietnam-war riots and the bombing on campus and told me he thought he'd go to divinity school. (Dare I presume to stay out of the service?) He was quickly accepted as an administrative intern and Nick was his mentor.

Randy agreed that I should keep my story in my desk drawer. Readers may get a negative perception that may be detrimental to the hospital's image. Okay. He's probably right.

When he left the office, I scribbled in jest what came out of my pen:

> Young man, you are so thin.
> Why do you wear long johns under your trousers?
> It makes you look bulky in your tight pants up to your
> Buttoned-up shirt and tie above.
> You need to be warmed,
> sustained, nurtured enough
> to face the world without protective padding.
>
> I'd like to play with you,
> give you a spark from one mature
> enough to give you more
> than thin young things can:
> some joy, some life to share
> from smoldering ashes that flame
> intently at the core
> of the earth, volcano's source.
> But I would break your bones
> And scare you with my power.
>
> Don't be afraid.
> I'm stronger, true,
> I'm wiser too;
> and I may take the challenge
> of warming you.

Jan on May 20, 1972

The Carnigans started looking for vacation land, searching through western and northern Wisconsin. The Dixons invited us to spend a November weekend on their Door County land. They'd host visitors in three trailers on their land and everyone congregated in the large garage to eat, play board games, and drink. Though the trips to the outhouse were chilly, I fell in love with the area, especially when the morning frost covered all in a silver dawn. I put my hand out to a fur tree branch as if to shake its hand and felt the warmth of the green bough as my body temperature melted its frosted glaze.

Stars shone brilliantly as we told stories around a huge campfire. One story Nick joked about was when he was a kid he sneaked up behind his sister and wrapped a live snake around her neck. She ran for home in terror; she was still terrified of snakes. He thrived on telling his guests his often-repeated stories, including tales about his gay uncle and how much he cared about him—rare information these days.

Later in their garage, during lots of drinking, Nick grabbed me roughly and pulled me on his lap. I laughed, stood up and crossed the room toward his wife. When Alex and I retired to our trailer, Alex told me, "If Nick does that again, I'll tell him to take your job and shove it."

"This is my job and I'll handle Nick."

We were lucky to find forty-four acres of Door County farmland with a rocky line with trees stretching across the top two/thirds of the land. In the midst of the front acres grew a tiny stand of birches that twisted their roots around ancient, exposed slabs of limestone. I saw myself walking there to sit and read and write in my notebooks. I instantly named it Mother's Woods. I would have my ashes stashed under one of the rock plates among the smooth-barked birches that seem to respond to my embraces. Yes, I embrace birch trees. I actually tried out the space and sat in the crotches of their clusters of split birch trunks, long-lived survivors against the wind and winter.

Without electricity and water, we improvised. Our camping equipment helped get us started. Before we built our outhouse, we cut a hole in the seat of a backless wooden chair, dug another hole about a couple feet deep into forest land, hung canvas from the trees and encouraged Pepper to escort us and stand by. I encouraged everyone to sing to warn others that privy's occupied. I recommended "Everything's Coming Up Roses," "Blue Skies Shining at Me," "On Top of Old Smoky," "Up a Lazy River," and most weather-appropriate, "Rain Drops Keep Falling on My Head." After Alex built a real outhouse, we painted it green and encouraged everyone to use the pencil tied with a long string to autograph and wax poetic on its unpainted interior.

The Raymond family who sold us the property paid Alex rent for the privilege of planting crops on the front acres. We'd also get jugs of water from the farmer, his wife and his family who always welcomed us when we came knocking on their back door.

We quickly bought a small trailer and a screened-in eating and cooking tent, but it was my idea to build a barn so we could entertain many friends. I was committed to having land for each of our children and their future. As Will Rogers once said, "Buy land. They ain't making any more of that stuff." We shopped for estimates to build the simple, large barn next year for about $5,000. There's no electricity, so we'll install gas tanks for energy and we investigated the state's forestry program to buy and plant a few thousand fragile and small evergreen trees around the rock piles, shrubs and wild grapevines that edge the acres. We're close to excellent fishing and swimming on Buckaroo Lake but we're still isolated when we're on our land.

There's room for more nature-oriented visitors now that the outhouse is in place.

Mother's Day weekend at our newly bought Door County land was the best Mother's Day I've ever experienced. Alex and Jenny, Matt and I teamed together, working in tandem to plant three thousand evergreen seedlings around the fence line of our very own forty-four acres. We filled the back of the station wagon with bags of seedlings that we bought from a Wisconsin agriculture program, drove the car forward bit by bit and followed its tracks in a straight line with one of us splitting open the earth with a spade and the other setting the seedling into the wedge and stomping back the dirt around each scrawny evergreen. We trusted Mother Nature to water them all.

We hired a local carpenter to build our barn. We had a loft put in half the inside space and we insulated and paneled the area beneath it to be heated with bottled gas when we're cold. Alex, Matt and his friend Karl added shingles to the massive roof and we all rolled sage green stain on the rest of the barn.

Another major accomplishment for me and my overcrowded church school was when the trustees, including Alex who was the chair, voted to purchase a two-family home two blocks from the church. I had pushed to find a permanent location for the upper grades since we started renting sites over the years at the YW, in a Catholic school and in The Pits, a basement party room at Scandinavian Brotherhood Hall reeking from Saturday night's beer, cigarette and cigar fumes. Alex made the arrangements for the home and reported to the board that acquisition and repair costs would be approximately $34,000 with a ten-year mortgage.

Many members like us donated furnishing, including our brown sectional sofa. Bea donated her mother's green couch for the upstairs living room, a blue chair and some of her paintings.

We called it Emerson House and I was the one who had keys.

Jan on May 29, 1972

My assignments are writing feature articles about women school bus drivers, women going back to school and other women's issues like topless dancing ordinances and abortion. My by-line stories are filling brown envelopes filed in the newspaper's library.

How about the manilla folder filling my files with some more family stories?

Alex Hartoon Carnigian

Dear Alex,
 You have been an inspiration to me,
 But would it not have been better
 To have loved as I love you
 And accepted each other in affirming ways.
 Jan

Alex Carnigian, seven years younger than his brother Peter, was born with the help of a midwife in their house on Jefferson Street. My Aunt Ora lived next door and thought Alex to be a sweet, quiet, polite boy, like his mother. Being so much younger than his siblings, Alex watched the angry discipline of his father toward his older sister and brothers and kept silent at his mother's knee.

Their firstborn, a daughter named Vartouhi (or Var), was one of 67 first-generation Armenian Americans born in Lakeshore Bay in 1922.

Alex's father, Hartoon, born in 1883 in eastern Turkey, where ancient Armenia once existed, died in 1943 on Alex's twelfth birthday. Alex told me he couldn't cry when his father died. His mother, Armenhue, was born in 1892 in the same Turkish area. She died of cancer at St. Agnes Hospital in 1960.

She liked me even if I was an "odar," a non-Armenian, "the other" and we'd sit on her back porch or at the kitchen table where she'd tell me a few details about the Armenian genocide that was too painful for her to tell her children.

The Father God of their Armenian orthodox religion laid a heavy hand on the men who carried out His patriarchal lineage, being vengeful, maybe violent if crossed. The man was the boss. And their obedient wives were charged to preserve and obey, that men are superior and women are subordinate. Yet the women filled their side of the church in their transplanted homeland after they were forced from home and family across Turkey to neighboring countries, North and South America and Europe.

They revered the faith. It held them together after families were separated and most were killed by the Turks from 1914 to 1923. World War I made stopping the massacre of Armenians and the relocation of survivors more complex. No wonder Armenians embrace as a family a person who lived near or in the same little village as their lost relatives at the ancient, dusty edge of Asia Minor. No wonder they obeyed the church fathers. Their paternalistic protection promised a good life after death that gave them strength to maintain their endangered species in this life.

Armenians fled when the Turkish government began a systematic massacre trying to destroy the family-oriented and educated Christian Armenians and their culture. The Turks killed thousands, shooting adults and stabbing babies with bayonets. The Turks accused them of helping the Russians and sent hundreds of thousands of men, women and children into the desert wasteland to die of starvation, exhaustion and sunstroke. Turkish soldiers would line up families, divide them and send each family member in separate groups in different directions so they would never find each other again.

Before the massacre ended, estimates of one-and-a-half million Armenians had died. Five hundred thousand more fled, seeking refuge in orphanages and relief organizations in many nations.

Alex's father left for America in the early years to escape being drafted into the Turkish army, where the Turks put Armenians in the front lines to be killed by the Allied Powers of World War I, primarily the British and Russian Empires and the French Republic. He entered the United States through the port of Boston, where he and his brother were hired by Lakeshore Bay foundries as soon as they stepped off the boat. Given train tickets to middle America, they filled jobs that no one else wanted.

Enough were hired at the same time to begin a homogeneous Armenian ethnic area. Though these early immigrant men had intended to return to their homeland, in time they made a permanent home in the United States when conditions became impossible in the Old Country. When they saved enough money, many men went back to Europe and Asia Minor to find Armenian wives among the refugees. Some would send a brother or a friend to find wives. There were mail-order wives, too.

Alex's father sent his brother who found each of them a wife working in a Catholic mission in Marseilles. One hour after Hartoon met Armenuhe at the dock in Boston, they were married and on the train to the brothers' jointly rented house on the 300 block of Wisconsin Avenue in a house that my Grandmother Bornofska had also lived in when she was first married. The old house had a dual concrete stairway and was surrounded by barren, inner-city brick and concrete. The Carnigian brothers and their new wives began to make an Armenian home in this American space far from their homeland.

Most of the Armenian women I knew were stocky, strong survivors wearing clean, printed cotton house dresses and when it was cold, they covered their rounded shoulders with heavy, black coats. As they aged, their dark, wavy hair grayed, shrouded in bakuskas, flowered, black-bordered scarves folded in a triangle and tied tightly under the chin. They tucked the scarf corners up and under the fabric edges to frame their ruddy, bold faces and deep brown, sad eyes…except for Alex's mother. She had photos showing her light, almost blonde hair. And her eyes were blue; a tired blue by the time I knew her. Alex inherited his eye color from her, except that his eyes are steely gray, more like the color of his mother's long hair tied in a bun.

More came as orphans and refugees. They married, made homes, raised children and established family life. They respected the home, education and the church with its rules that were set in ancient stone, rules that were orderly and dogmatic with traditions that gave them stability in strange surroundings.

I'd heard that after toddler Vartouhi started crawling and almost fell down the outside concrete stairs, the family bought their little home with a yard for a garden. It was near other Armenians, close to Armenian grocery stores and within walking distance of the foundry.

Two Armenian congregations with strong political differences were maintained, one meeting at the Episcopal Church until the members could start St. Gregory's Church. The second faction occupied a tiny frame church, St. Basil's. Both churches are located near each other but were politically and religiously split centuries ago and still are today.

The homesickness and loneliness for their lost families and a murdered culture were slowly substituted with simple homes and garden harvests of freshly picked cucumbers, sometimes eaten off the vine to be savored on the spot after the soil had been rubbed off, with the men's nightly cartoon card games and with the women sewing altar cloths for the church gatherings. Many learned English from family service programs, from reading The *Bay View News* and bargaining for produce at the outdoor farmers' market one long block south from Alex's home.

Together they began a whole new crop of Armenian-American offspring who dutifully went to Armenian school, somehow replacing the lost fathers and mothers, brothers and sisters and children killed in the first wholesale genocide in modern history.

They were alive. They had new families. They had their churches. They had hope.

CHAPTER THREE

Bea Louise Holmes Lindberg

"Whatever you think you can do or believe you can do, begin it. Action has magic, grace and power in it."
Johann Wolfgang van Goethe

"There's no such word as 'Can't!'"
Omaha Coleman Holmes

Bea on June 11, 1964

I took my kids to the Unitarian church this morning. My friend and neighbor Marilyn Murak suggested I try there after I told her I walked out of my mother's Methodist Sunday school when the teacher told the kids that the devil tempted them.

I think I surprised Jan Carnigian, the worship leader, when I brought Josh and Jim into her group and sat down in the back row to hear what she'd say. I guess most parents drop off their kids and go on to church. I watched and listened. The children started singing.

> "From all that dwell below the skies
> Let faith and hope with love arise;
> Let beauty, truth and good be sung
> Through every land, by every tongue."

The children were encouraged to talk about people who have worked for peace and they closed the little worship service singing "Where Have All the Flowers Gone" before they went to their separate classes.

Josh enjoyed his fourth-grade class where he learned about the Egyptian pharaoh Akhenaton who honored his wife as an equal partner and worshipped one god, Ra, the Sun God. I liked that. Josh had Mrs. Carnigian for his teacher and I was surprised that both boys liked their classes.

Bea on June 14, 1965

I soon got tired of sermons, so I volunteered to teach Sunday school. Jan handed me *Stonehenge Decoded* by Gerald Hawkins. "I watched a PBS television program on Sunday that touched my soul," she explained. "It was on Stonehenge—that place in England where the druids were supposed to have built something astrological."

You mean astronomical? Yes? Places like Stonehenge have intrigued me, too."

"I checked this book out of the library and I thought we could consider this subject for one of our classes. Why don't you review it and if you like it, we can submit the idea to the Religious Education committee for approval."

"I can do that."

Within the week, I'd devoured the book and built a semester's curriculum on Stonehenge, its history and its meaning for us. Soon my new church third-graders were building the monolithic structure out of soap in the kitchen, creating model solar systems above the classroom and casting equinox and solstice sunrises with their flashlights shining through the Stonehenge heel stone.

Women often conform to others' expectations, but at our UU church school, we have ourselves a lifeline of individual women's creativity and fun and who, like me, couldn't tolerate the intellectual sermonizing upstairs with the adults. Instead, we built a subculture downstairs with the kids and the liberal UU religious education curriculum when one is offered. And if we aren't happy with what was offered through the denomination, we made up our own. Together we became a successful creative force quite independent from the minister and the church Board of Trustees that provides us with a $100 budget each year.

Most UU churches close during the summer, but Jan is having us meet at Pritchard Park every Thursday. We bring the kids who play on the swings and in the woods while we plan next year's program.

To get better acquainted, Jan asked us to share something about our lives starting with our parents. I typed mine and I'll read some of it aloud and keep the whole story for my personal history. Though I write a daily sentence or two in my little datebook, like my mother does, typing these details gives me a chance to write about family, and my kids will enjoy reading this when they're adults.

I was born on May 25, 1930.
My mother's name is Omaha Agnes Coleman Holmes. Her name is Omaha because she was born there in 1899. My dad calls her Oma and I call her "Oh Ma." Mother's sister is named Nevada because that's where she was born. A third sister lucked out. Florence was born in Florence, Iowa.

Oma looks like Ingrid Bergman. She's creative and determined. She can do anything! She's designed my clothes, making the patterns and sewing me into high fashion. She knits and crochets, and makes dolls, doilies, and ceramics. She can look at another's piece of clothing or a gewgaw or gimcrack and make it herself for hundreds of bazaars to benefit her organization.

My father is Charles Everett Holmes, who was born in Turo, Iowa, in 1898. Charles, also known as Ducky, is fun, inventive and dreadfully straightforward. Ducky's entertaining when he doesn't drink too much. He's a retired electrician and supervisor of the service and repair department at Commonwealth Edison in Chicago, so our family never worried about The Depression. He entertains us with jokes and stories, reciting poems like "Hiawatha" and singing "Abdul a Bull Bull Ameir," often helped by a jug of wine or a fifth of hard liquor.

Ducky has a terrible temper that isn't helped when he drinks. He drank a lot at home when I was a kid and he still does. He has the most incredible swear word vocabulary that I inherited. Dad said when we'd be working together on a project, "If you can't make something work, swear at it and it will work fine."

Oma is a homemaker—an authentic homemaker because she helped my dad build a log cabin and a ranch home. They bought Door County property on the Green Bay shore. They designed the log cabin plans and cut most of the trees from the land. They stripped off the bark and set them up for the walls and ceiling beams. Their friends pitched in and helped them erect the main structure. My older brother, Cal, and I helped too, spending many weekends working on the cabin.

We have home movies of the entire building process.

Mother thought we should have a natural stone fireplace. She read books and said, "I can do that!" And she did. The fireplace started with a metal liner and Dad was her assistant, carried her stone and mixed the mortar. We found the stone on the property and dragged a trailer around beautiful Door County looking for more. She built the eight-foot-wide fireplace with her own hands, mortaring the joints barehanded when she grew impatient with her gloves. The lye in the mortar ate away the top layers of skin on her fingers. The result was an impressive stone fireplace with a two-piece flat slab stone mantel about four inches thick. It worked wonderfully and kept us warm. After filling the chinks to caulk the logs with ropey oakum, the cabin always smelled of fireplace wood, ashes and the pleasant tarry smell. The cabin still stands today.

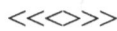

Margery Ann Manley

"I'll do my thing and you do your thing.
I am not in this world to live up to your expectations,
and you are not in this world to live up to mine.
You are you and I am I;
If by chance we find each other, it's beautiful—
if not, it can't be helped."

Fritz Perls

Marge on June 16, 1965

OK. I'll tell you all a story about my parents.

Nina and my father owned a barbershop and I still smell the place with its manly aftershave lotions and see his white enamel chairs with black seats and silver trim, the worn leather strap that he'd use to sharpen his razors. Living upstairs of the shop, my mom and my half-sister and I'd hear the way the men talked about sports, politics, women and sex through the heating vents in the floor.

I also remember when I was a little girl and asked my mother why my sister and I looked so different. She's tall and bulky; I'm short and slimmer. She explained that my sister had a different father. They married and had my sister but he womanized, drank and gambled and Nina divorced him after three years—and saw him murdered for not paying his gambling debts in a gangland-type shooting on Chicago's church steps. My mother hasn't spoken much of it since, but I can't even imagine how scared and insecure she must have felt. It's a good thing she met my dad and moved to Wisconsin.

Did I surprise you with that story? You all think Nina is such a sweetie; how could she lose her husband in such a violent act? I've lost my husband too, but in a violently emotional way.

I interrupted after a pause from Marge. "I remember a UU Supper Club when we first met you and your husband and other church couples our age." And then I took over the conversation. "When Alex and I were students in Madison, we visited the Frank Lloyd Wright-designed Unitarian church, but the sermon was too intellectual. My American literature class on campus about Unitarian thinkers was more enlightening.

"Before your Supper Club night, Marge, Alex and I visited our Universalist Church, heard Curtis Harris preach and discovered the link between Universalists and Unitarians. You must have been downstairs with the church school kids because the congregation upstairs all seemed to be over seventy years old. Alex looked up at the light bulbs hanging high overhead and told me that if we joined this church, he'd be the only one physically able to change those bulbs.

"Rev. Harris visited me at Lakeshore Med's maternity ward after my Matt was born and invited us to Supper Club. I admired you from our first meeting, Marge. Your laughter, direct manner and openness attracted me and that motivated me to have us become members in 1960. But soon after we became friends, your husband took you and your mischievous son away from us. Was I surprised when two years later I saw you holding the new baby Timothy at the Mall and you told me you were divorced and living here with your boys?"

"I was truly happy, Jan, to get such a warm reception from you. I didn't know how others would react—that I'd gotten a divorce from that bastard—and also had my baby Tim, my ex-'s final gift to me. And I now raise two boys as a single parent. Good thing my parents are helping me out."

Slightly stunned, I apologized to Marge, "Sorry, I took over your life story. Let's hear more from you."

"That's all right, Jan, you helped me focus on the hard facts.

Bea on June 23, 1965

This morning, we shared a memory about childhood friends. I thought I'd lighten up the gals right away.

My friend Millie's house was across the street.
When I was about five, Millie, who was nearly two years older, taught me how to masturbate. What a wonderful discovery since I was able to achieve orgasm during this process, one activity bringing great independence that I value all my life.
Millie again changed my life later when on a whim, she stuck a garden hose up my nose and turned it on full blast to see what effect it would have.
Well, I always say, you win some and you lose some!
We're not meeting because some are on vacation and Jan has a heavy-duty work schedule helping her dad build floats for the 4th of July parade. I'm keeping on with my writing anyway. Once my kids are out playing and I get to typing, my mind keeps going and I can't

stop. Maybe I can submit some of these stories to my Southport Writers' Club or freelance some to a woman's magazine. I'd change the names, of course, and I'd have to delete some of the details.

When Jan talked about her travels in Germany and the rest of western Europe in the mid-50s when her husband was an Army lieutenant, I couldn't help but compare my adventures. I was busy having babies: Joshua (Josh), 7 pounds, 6 1/2 ounces, on March 2, 1955; James (Jim), 7 pounds, 10 1/2 ounces, on June 21, 1956; Jill Elizabeth, 8 pounds, 2 ounces, on January 6, 1958; and Joel (Joey), my biggest baby born at 9 pounds, 1 ounce, on August 13, 1959.

How's that to brag about? Good thing Joey was my last one.

And I'm still busy raising them. That's my top priority.

It's amazing I didn't get pregnant before marriage and then when I married, I had the babies I wanted right away.

Before all that, I tried college. I wasn't unattractive but painfully shy—and a virgin. I went for two years and graduated with an associate degree with honors.

I joined a sorority with great pleasure and success including a triad friendship with Peg and Maryann. I dated, went to formal dances and practically went steady with a handsome friend named Joe, who, in retrospect, must have been gay. At the end of two years, I was still a virgin.

Though it was two hours of subways each way and I worked part-time at Woolworth's record department, I transferred to Wisconsin Teachers College for a hellish semester. My dad was after me to quit. "What are you going to school for? Get a job. Get married. Get on with it!" So I gave up. I went to work at an insurance company for three years through several promotions and salary increases before I became so bored and was fired for coming in late.

I was twenty-one and bought my own car—a black '49 Studebaker with red trim. Peg and I drove west for 6,141 miles in sixteen days through Carlsbad Caverns, Juarez, Mexico, the Grand Canyon, Los Angeles, San Francisco, Lake Tahoe, Salt Lake, Yellowstone and the Black Hills. When Peg's driving didn't seem safe enough to me, I took over and drove all but fifty of those miles.

Back to night school for a year of French, I formed another triad with Shirley and Inez. We called ourselves The Rowdy Girls and proceeded to try to live up to our image. We picked up the guys in my car. We drank Rumtinis—that's four fingers of rum in a glass—we sang and caroused. We'd sail in Shirley's boat and sometimes got towed on the ironing board at her parents' property on some lake in Michigan.

One night Shirley and I fooled around, kissing and whatever. Shirley stopped me, saying, "Bea, I don't see anything wrong with this. I'm enjoying it, but until you have had sex with a guy like I've had lots of times—and you have not had any—I don't think you should do this."

Somewhere along here, I took Shirley's advice and lost my virginity—and after that, with more than one guy.

With my mother's dress designer skills, I became a handsome woman in a slim, black-velvet, sleeveless dress with a short, black velvet jacket with a red satin lining. In one of the two pockets high up on the breast, I carried a slim silver cigarette case my mother gave me for Christmas. The case had a built-in lighter that snapped a flame when you closed the cover after retrieving a cigarette. I was a femme fatale in this getup, proven by a liaison at a motel with an experienced divorced man having the best sex of my life up to then.

Meanwhile, my mother kept asking, "Why don't you get married? I don't have grandchildren and all my friends have grandchildren."

In October 1954, my car conked out on my way to an Air Force air show near Oshkosh. I pulled into a gas station, lifted up the hood and began fooling around with the carburetor. Ducky taught me how when I had car problems at home. I'd put on a pair of overalls and climb under the car, fix it and get back in. This time I was dressed up and under the hood and along came Jake Lindberg, so masculine, handsome and sweet. He said the usual line, "Are you having trouble? Do you want to go and have a drink?" So we went off and had a drink. Then we went off in his car and had sex and for three months that's all we did. We would date and go off and have sex somewhere.

Jake was in construction and drove a dump truck hauling concrete to build expressways. He was going off to Florida over the winter months. I told him if he didn't take me with him, I wouldn't be here when he came back. He said OK. I always said I married Jake because I knew we would breed well. So we went to Naples, Florida, were married by Judge Jolly and moved into Jake's bedroom in his parents' house. I started to worry when I wasn't pregnant right away. About a year later, I had Josh, my first child.

From the maternity ward, we went to live with my parents, but I was so nervous. I couldn't breastfeed. My mother didn't approve and I had to quit. I thought I was starving my firstborn to death. We moved back to Jake's family. I'd get up at 3:30 a.m., make Jake's lunch, kiss him off to work and fall back to sleep until the baby woke up.

I must have been bored out of my gourd. I actually painted by the numbers with Jake. Oh yes. I painted the crib and I knitted for the baby, plus a sweater for Jake that had such long sleeves, like Dopey, that he couldn't wear it.

I enjoyed his Swedish parents, Sari and Hilding, who had their two children born in Chicago and wanted to give them good American names, Joan and Jake, but they couldn't pronounce the Js and called them Yoan and Yake. Tightwad Hilding was saving his money as a house painter for their retirement, so Sari worked as a cleaning lady to earn extra money.

Joel, our fourth, was conceived in a room where Jake and I slept with the three kids. I was afraid to put the kids upstairs because they would be too far away and I couldn't hear them if they needed me. Nevertheless, Joey was conceived next to the two boys in bunk beds and Jill in a bassinet next to the freezing window, where she caught a serious ear infection.

That's when my mother and I shopped for a mobile home. Jake liked it and we bought ourselves a brand new eight-foot-wide, forty-foot-long, two-bedroom unit and put it at a trailer park in Des Plaines and lived there for three years.

That's where Marilyn Murak and I became friends. She lived next to us and had four kids too, but she started earlier at sixteen and had to get married to Steve. My kids' names all started with a J; her kids' names started with a K. We are still friends, including our kids and we go boating together.

Jake and I finally moved back into Jake's dad's house that he was supposed to be selling to us. Widowed Hilding lived there alone, but he also had a little cabin where he was going to retire on the Lake Michigan side of Door County across the opposite Green Bay side of the peninsula where my parents had built their cabin.

What we didn't know was that Jake's father came with the deal on his house. We lived there for six months. I almost went mad trying to adjust to that man. He declared himself "a king in my own home" and was a vicious, stingy bastard. He was retired and home all day with me, where I was tending to children and trying to make a home for my family. I never could do anything right for Hilding. He directed my every move, how to clean the cabinets, how to cook the food. He told my kids how to eat. At last, I told Jake we had to move, even though Hilding was selling the house cheap.

Hilding put his hands on me once as if he owned his son's wife as well as his own. It was so bad I even resorted to hiding a bottle of spirits in the glossy, fake-marble green wicker bathroom laundry hamper so I could lift my spirits when I went in there to relieve myself. I'd take a drink and say, "I'm not going to let that bastard get me down."

We found a new subdivision built with pre-fab houses in Southport. We liked it and picked out our large lot on a cul de sac. We chose a house plan without a basement because we could afford it, a tiny house with a living room, kitchen, three bedrooms and a bath. The kitchen's so small when all six of us ate at the only table in the house, the built-in oven door dropped down over the east end of the table and someone had to move so I could get the casserole or whatever out of the oven. In a tiny closet room off the kitchen, I built a sort of workshop with shelves for a pantry above the little desk. You could close the door of that closet and have a little privacy, too.

I've been a faithful wife to Jake and a professional parent to our children.

Anna Spence

"Muddy waters let stand become clear."
Ira Progoff

Anna on July 6, 1965

Jan! I waited until you came back from church camp so you could hear about my mentor—Your mother, Mildred.

My father, Mike, and his two brothers came here from Sicily when he was 17. The D'Acquistos were in the tavern business, "The Three Brothers." When my father was 35 and couldn't find an American woman good enough to marry, he went back to Sicily for an arranged marriage to my mother. I was born exactly nine months later and when I was one, the three of us returned to Lakeshore Bay. My mother was pregnant with my sister Marie and we lived near The Three Brothers.

My sisters Feona and Gena were born soon after. Then my mother was bedridden at home when I was five and was soon sent to the TB Sanatorium. She died three years later during the Crash of '29 and my father told me that I was Mother now. I did what I had to do and what I was told to do.

When I went to Roosevelt High School, we moved upstairs to the tavern. That's when I found that your mother and father were good friends with my father. Your dad must have painted some beer signs, but other connections were made among us. Your aunt rented the back room for Ora's Bingo and all your family came to help sell bingo cards, check the winning ones and serve drinks and food. When Ora hollered out the numbers and "Bingo," we could hear her out in front, up the stairs and outside the building.

You'd come along too, Jan, and soon you'd come upstairs to play with Feona and fall asleep until bingo ended. Your mother's good friend Edie was also a chum of my father's lady friend, Katie May.

You were only a kid and I hardly noticed when you were there, but your mother became so important to me. She would talk with me and try to make me laugh. She said I had a pretty smile and should show it more. She tried to give me the confidence I needed, especially when I became the class valedictorian and had to make a graduation speech. But most of all, she made my graduation dress. She asked me, "Would you like to wear a blue fabric that would bring out your eyes or brown that would complement your hair?" No one had ever singled me out with such thoughtfulness. And she was an important woman, a woman in business and a float builder. Yet she took time for me.

Ha! Then years later, when I needed a church school for my four children, I walked through our sanctuary's double doors and you swept me up hollering "Annie!" and put me right on the job of teaching Sunday school. I picked kindergarten with the little ones because my youngest daughter was so shy and needed me.

I jumped up and gave Anna a hug, "I never realized my mother meant that much to you. I do remember you, so serious all the time, ironing in a dark kitchen with electric cord extensions plugged into the single light bulb ceiling socket hanging over the table. I remember the windows slightly open overlooking the roofs and the hot radiators that burned me when I touched them. And did you know that I was inspired by your sister when she came to our house one afternoon to ask my mother to write a letter of reference so she could apply for college at the University of Wisconsin? I never knew anyone who went to college, let alone one who'd think my mother's recommendation would be so important. You are a sister to me, Anne, with your calm inspiration, being so faithful, reliable, trustworthy and loving us all—and you have taught us all how to hug each other.

Jan on July 20, 1965

When our small city was a hotbed of labor turmoil in the late 20s and early 30s, our family decorated union-organized Labor Day parade cars and floats. Their first float was for my parents' union, the Painters, Decorators and Paperhangers of America, Local 10.

It was spectacular for those days, a paper-covered, framed-based diorama over a beat-up farm trailer embellished with crepe paper flowers, garlands and fringe made by Aunt Ora and Uncle Pete and friends working around the dining room table all winter for this float and many more. (And when they were working away building and decorating the floats, teenage Cousin Toots would babysit me until I was about four.)

But the float's greater impact was having its determined union members marching behind it. During those years, every union had its own decorated car with its signature sign, most often made by my father, or a float and every union member marched in the Labor Day parade—or else.

Starting in the 1930s, Lakeshore Bay was spilt by crushing labor-management problems leading to strikes. In Washington, D.C., President Roosevelt initiated his New Deal labor laws and gave labor the power to negotiate and fight for their interests. This discord left the city divided into two strong enemies, labor and management. The conflict reached its height in 1934 when union members went on strike simultaneously at six of the largest industrial plants. Lakeshore Bay, being percentage-wise one of the largest industrialized cities in the US, was a focal point for labor and a spearhead for national union organization." A national commentator called Lakeshore Bay "Little Moscow."

Mildred, in her prime, would motivate Barney and others to work to improve the lives of men and women through the labor movement. In addition to her many meeting with her labor friends, I remember tagging along with her Trade Union Women organized to bring food to the strikers carrying signs, holding sit-down strikes, and picketing for weeks and months around the now-quiet factory buildings.

R.C. "Rick" Rose, a daily columnist for The *Bay View News*, granted me an interview in 1953 for a UW-Madison journalism term paper. (I got an A+ but who cares.) Rose credits union leaders, local manufacturers, businessmen and city government officials for bringing Lakeshore Bay's turbulent factions together to start a 4th of July Celebration and heal the city's labor-management strife causing a series of crushing strikes.

But Rick Rose missed something historically important and I didn't realize it until I found a faded *Bay View News* clipping in my files from May 6, 1990. It referred to a banquet sponsored by the Women's Trade Union League at the best hotel with a "Bury the Hatchet" theme. Then I remembered curling up on the hotel's balcony with my Cousin Toots to watch my mother and all the ladies and gentlemen dressed up and making speeches, striving to bury the hatchet of strife between industry and labor. Mildred and her Women's Trade Union League friends inspired those influential people to come together and expand the newly formed Lakeshore Bay's 4th of July Goodwill Celebration.

All at the banquet signed a real hatchet with goodwill towards all

Mother was one of two women chosen to be on the first Goodwill Committee. Perhaps she was chosen because of leading the "Bury the Hatchel" banquet and because she decorated the best parade floats for Labor Day parades.

"Starting the Golden Age of Floats" A Mother's Day Salute by Jan Anthony on May 10, 1989

Floral paper, wood lathe and staple guns–those are items I recall when I remember my mother, Mildred Anthony, on the 4th of July. Hot canned chicken soup in July for quick energy, laughter among people working together, tears under tension during deadline hours, and exhaustion mixed with excitement when Lakeshore Bay's parade started to move. It was all worth it as crowds cheered our floats.

My mother was the spark that energized my dad, Barney, and relatives, friends and me into a team of float builders. They could take an artist's concept from a sketch and make it live as a colorful, moving showpiece that stirred and entertained many thousands of cheering people.

In the beginning, my mother and relatives spent winters making flowers out of crepe paper to decorate their first floats. Then they bought ready-made flowers and petal paper.

I was part of the action most of my life. When I was really young, I would play around them and nap on float paper in their boxes. When I was able to help, I'd fetch things, fill staple guns, run errands, mind the shop, and squeeze into spaces inside floats to pin where no one else could fit. I was expected to help or to stay out of trouble after the parade when they dismantled each float and saved much of the paper.

I'd watch my mother work. Long float pins stuck on her loosely fitting blouse were ready to tack down a loose paper corner. Her fingertips were covered with masking tape for protection from the hundreds of pins she'd apply to chicken wire frames or she used staples to attach floral paper over lumber. She'd be dusty from crawling under float framework on factory floors, lumber yards and loading docks around the clock if necessary.

My mother and Ruby Jefferson were the only two women who served on the original Fourth of July Goodwill committee of twenty-three business and labor leaders to heal conflicts from the many strikes. Though I was just a kid, I remember being impressed when I saw her being filmed for a movie made at one of those meetings.

She was a vital woman, strong and determined. If a carpenter wouldn't build to her specifications, she'd pick up her tools and do it herself. (Then there were few power tools and none to use where we worked.) A warm and creative woman, she could build floats that turned a plodding old farm wagon into Cinderella's carriage with its stallions when dairy delivery horses pulled those majestic floats.

A vulnerable woman, she endured long hours of labor, but her need for more energy could not be renewed indefinitely.

An effective leader, during WWII, she led her crew to create inspiring patriotic floats like Betsy Ross with her 13-Star-Spangled Banner or the Liberty Bell. My dad was in the Navy then and when he returned, she retired and I was expected to decorate my first floats. I was 15. My first production featured a huge red rose to hold a beauty queen. Initially, I didn't think I could do it, but knowing I was Mildred Anthony's daughter, I knew I would do it. That beautiful float was my tribute to her.

I have always gained strength from the positive inspiration of a mother such as mine. She died after a long illness and extensive hospitalization. With many images to remember her by, I like to remember her at her best–when she was Lakeshore Bay's greatest float decorator and I was her daughter.

CHAPTER FOUR

Bea on August 4, 1965

Did we save the most controversial topic until the end of our sessions: "Describe an early sexual experience." Well, here goes.

    I had fun hanging around Mary Lou's house with an older sister and two older brothers. I liked her mother too, but I was mixed up about her father who took a liking to me. I sensed something was wrong. I was too young to know what the problem was. It would happen when the neighborhood gang was playing in Mary Lou's basement. Her father would come and sit on the stairs and call for me to come up to sit by him. Then he would proceed to put his hand down and around my small back, into my underpants and massage my clitoris. This was a pleasant feeling, but it seemed so wrong. I felt awful and creepy and yet, it felt good. The other kids would say, "Hey, Bea, come on and play with us," and I'd try to get away. I felt like an insect pinned in a display, but I would stay for a few more minutes near that man. I didn't want to make a scene; I didn't want to leave his touch; I hated his every move. How mixed up I was. What a dilemma!
    I don't know often or how long this went on, but one day I rebelled when my parents were to go to an American Legion

Convention in New York and planned to leave me at Mary Lou's house.

"I won't stay at Mary Lou's house!"

"Why?"

"Mary Lou's father is creepy! He always touches me. And one night, when I stayed at Mary Lou's, her father came into the bedroom where Mary Lou and I were sharing a bed. He sat on my side. He touched me and then he made me touch his thing."

My appalled mother couldn't believe it. Mary Lou's mother was her best friend. I don't know, but maybe she didn't believe me either.

One day when I came home from school for lunch, my mother acted weird. Something else was weird too. I noticed that the bathroom door next to the kitchen was almost closed. Mom gave me my lunch, but it became apparent that something else was on the menu other than bologna sandwiches. She started asking me questions about why I didn't want to stay with the Mary Lou's during the American Legion Convention. I didn't like the way the questioning went, but I answered truthfully even though the subject made me squirm. I had to say the whole thing over and over again. Finally, my mother was satisfied.

And then it was revealed. Mary Lou's mother was sequestered in the bathroom listening to my testimony.

When I found that out, I felt betrayed twice. Nothing ever happened to her father except that I didn't have to stay there when my parents went away. It seemed to me that I ended up being a suspect, not him.

Mary Lou grew up and became a nun.

Jan Delores Anthony Carnigian

"Some seek love, some seek fame,
But I made a dash after both."
The Polaris Yearbook, 1949
Theodore Roosevelt High School

Jan on August 10, 1965

The subject of sex has always interested me. I don't think I was actually molested when I was four or five, but one of our boarders, Uncle Al, had me naked with him while he was supposed to be babysitting me. Nothing much happened that I remember but I still remember that room.

The next day I told my mother and I never saw Uncle Al again.

My sex lessons advanced quickly, finding out more from three Italian brothers on Hill Street in the back bushes of the Episcopalian church behind their house. They had their pants down and I dropped my coveralls and sat on one of their laps. My girl-friend Ruthie was supposed to do that too, but she ran home and told her mother.

It's amazing how you can walk half a block away from a scene with a puzzled smile on your face and by the time you're home, your mother's waiting with a frown.

While their parents probably were scolding the others, I was getting an earnest lesson in self-respect and the functions of sexual and reproductive organs. My mother had saved a *Life* magazine article on how babies were born and the two of us sat down and shared it. I learned what the genitals were for and what happens if you misuse the privileges of having them. My mother's calm attitude about sex was comforting and I wasn't punished for having a normal curiosity. But I was told to stay away from those boys—and the bushes. I'll bet the punished boys started again to pick other forbidden fruit they were supposed to be denied.

The other women in our circle sympathized, even chuckled about our early sexual experiences, but they begged off about sharing their early sexual escapades, especially Anna who kept quiet and suggested we go back to developing the Sunday school curriculum for the rest of the sessions.

Jan on August 15, 1965

Most parents think we have the greatest influence on our children, but my friends and their families have been as important to me. As an only child, I'd adopt families.

I was indifferent to my school experiences but I learned as early as kindergarten that the boys had better toys, like four-foot building logs to construct castles for kings and knights and forts to play cowboys and Indians.

But I thrived with my Hill Street gang with my best friend Ruthie and her family. I'd eat lunch at their kitchen table with their five kids squeezed together on benches. Ruthie's nurturing Danish mother, who was a family friend, would hardly notice me, only one more hungry kid.

I don't ever remember making any of my many adopted families angry with me. I needed them and I wanted to please them, especially their moms.

More than being an only child, I must have needed to adopt families because my parents worked together in their sign-writing business and building floats for Labor Day parades.

Jan on September 23, 1965

I've got a lot to be thankful for despite being born under tragic circumstances leading to my birth on November 14, 1931.

But I was conceived in love, a once-in-a-lifetime love that captivated my father, freed my mother from her mismatched marriage and alienated many. Yes, adultery, conflict, lust and extra-marital intimacies exist in many family histories.

I read somewhere that the egg that made me begin traveling around as an ovum in my mother's ovaries since my mother was an ovum in my grandmother's womb. I'm not sure about that, but now I need the right father—and the right day. It was Barney Anthony and it could have been Valentine's Day, 1931.

Mildred Kreuger and Carl B. Anthony were married on January 1, 1930, at his mother's Evangelical Lutheran Church. That may have been one of the few times my parents went to church together. Mildred had been a married woman with a son, Richard, Jr. when she and Barney looked at each other and fell in love. What could they do? It was meant to be.

Her marriage to Dick Kreuger was a mistake. She was sixteen, from a busy little city. He was a farmer who came to the city to earn factory money; she was a shoe factory worker with a feisty, free spirit. "Remember, Jan," my mother told me when I was a teen, "you don't have to get married just because someone touches you."

On February 14, 1931, Barney handed his wife a Valentine's package. "I found this for you, Muddie," as she opened her present—an artificial mother of pearl, yellow-marbled and amber-edged hand mirror that reflected her smiling face. "I'm sorry it's second-hand," he whispered lovingly, "and it's not engraved with M for you, but it's etched with an S and that stands for Sweetheart."

And they made love without worrying about birth control. They were ready to have a child of their own whether they could afford one or not. The Depression. Little work. They were poor and living in a back upper flat on Marquette Street north of State Street behind Roman's Fish Market across from Maritato's beer and liquor warehouse.

Mildred adored her husband Barney, her son Richard and me growing inside her warm, vibrant body. I was strong and I was growing. My half-brother was happily expecting a baby sister or brother. My father loved me and Mother and Richard and he tried to get work—but only in his trade.

I'd listen from my womb, where learning begins. I heard stomach rumblings, the swooshing blood pulses, the endless heartbeat echoes and the laughing voices of my loving parents and Richard. I moved and floated weightless and secure. Content with multiplying my cells and expanding my brain, spine, genitals, legs, arms, toes, and face, my mouth could taste the fluids I lived and played in and my searching fingers reaching to explore.

But something abruptly changed. I was transported by my mother running to a dreadful, agonizing site. She saw Richard, her Junie, being hit by a truck; and after her heartbeat pounded in that run to his side, the movement around me diminished to a heartbreaking throb. In sorrow now, slower, heavy heartbeats replaced the expectant rhythm of love and anticipation.

How do maternal emotions influence a preborn's psyche and does that influence retain its power for life?

The stronger movements now are mine as my knees, elbows and head strain against the womb's restraints. On the outside, rolling waves appear under her black mourning dress. Whatever nourishment was there for us, I sapped into myself. The spectral hollows of her cheeks and around her eyes contrasted with her expanding waistline. I could not give in. I had to grow. I had to live. I had to be.

Aware now of angry noise beyond my insular universe, discord bounced off the walls and vibrated against my taut sphere: quarrelsome accusing voices, scuffling sounds, eruptions from outside me. Immediately after Richard's funeral, my mother's ex- and his family confronted my parents about their affair and blamed my mother for Richard's death.

The heartbeat thump accelerated and I felt compression from her retching. Her emotional pain and sobbing sound contracted against me.

Soon I would free myself from this frail and brittle frame.

Mildred Lueckfeld Kreuger Anthony

> "O Sacred Head, now wounded,
> With grief and shame weighed down
> Now scornfully surrounded
> With thorns, Thine only crown.
> O Sacred Head, what glory;
> What bliss, till now was Thine!
> Yet, tho' despised and gory,
> I joy to call Thee mine."
>
> *The Lutheran Hymnal, Hymn 172*

Mildred writes in a tablet on June 14, 1931

I'm not thinking clearly but I must write this to sort out what happened. I have so much pain. My precious Richard was taken from me—on June 1, just when our lives were blooming again. How can I go on? Am I really to blame? How can this be? I'm a good woman. Just because I fell in love? How can love be to blame?

That's what the Kreugers hollered at me after Richard's funeral. Self-righteous Dick and his parents actually tromped up the stairs to our little flat and pounded on our door, but Barney wouldn't let them in. They shouted at us that our behavior caused God's wrath that took my Richard away from me.

I didn't love Richard's father. And I hated living on his farm for eight years. I had to leave him and when Luella and her son, Eugene, drove here from California with my teenage sister Emmalyn, I had to get in that car with my little Junie and drive back with her to California to get far enough away from Richard Kreuger Senior.

Cars and trucks. Cars and trucks rumble about on our busy corner. Why did Junie step off the curb just then to cross the street to come to me? He's eight years old. He should have known to look both ways. When I screamed, everyone looked and saw what I saw. And the driver was drunk. I know he was. He came from the beer warehouse. He was drunk.

Pronounced dead at St. Agnes. My little boy.

The *Bay View News* reported that Joe Connor, the driver of the truck, said he was driving south on Marquette Street and he noticed an automobile from the west side. The boy was running alongside that automobile, dashed in front of his truck and was hit by the right front fender.

This was at 7:35 p.m. I went in the ambulance with Richard and he passed away from a fracture of the skull at 8:30.

The paper even wrote, "Richard was a pupil of Lincoln School, a bright, active boy and a general favorite with teachers and fellow students."

The funeral was at the church where Barney and I had been married a year ago last January. Barney bought a pillow for Richard's head that had "Sonny" embroidered on it. All I have now are Western Union telegrams and letters—and bills, including one to St. Agnes Hospital for $15 and another big one to the funeral home for $319. And flower receipts. We had to buy a cemetery plot—a shared one with another family that was less expensive. My green Mona Lisa stocking box will keep these papers safe in one place.

Grandma Emma wrote a note from Berkeley on June 2.

Just a few words of comfort to you and Barney. We all feel so bad for you. I can't explain. I know how you feel when one takes a piece of your heart. It's too bad it had to happen. They called them cars Devil's Wagons.

That's what they are. Can't be too careful. I sit here with my heart in my throat all the time, but the Lord always has a hand in it and we don't know for what good it is. He is well off and dies as a little Angel. You don't have to worry any more. You don't know what might have been in store for him. As it is now, one has no pleasure out of children after they're big. If it's not one thing, it's the other. Now console yourself with the Lord and take him as your Guide and Master and you'll bear it all well. One thing I'm glad you have, Barney and don't let Dick say one word to you about it. You can be glad you have him with you now. He doesn't have to try to hold you from anything. I know it will be hard. I've never lost one of mine, but it hurts me as much to lose my grandchildren. I sat down Sunday night and was going to write Jr. a letter. Please let me know how you are in health. I hope you control your nerves and not let them run away. Pa feels for you too. So that's all we can do for you at present.

Love from all,
Pa, Ma, Sis, Bros."

Oh, Ma. How I fought in the courts to keep Richard from his father and with Barney and me—and now he's gone from all of us.

Mildred on June 15, 1931

I'm five months pregnant. How will I cope? And my little baby will never know what a wonderful brother he or she would have had.

God giveth and He taketh away. But I don't deserve this. We don't deserve this. I have all the proof here that I'm a good woman. The papers in my brown legal folder prove it. I married Dick on April 2, 1921, divorced him on October 16, 1928, and married Barney on January 1, 1930. Nothing wrong with that? Wasn't it enough to fight for custody and child support? Now must I sue the driver who killed my son?

Here's proof of my custody rights. "February 15, 1929, Citation, signed by Harvey Stanke that Mrs. Mildred Kreuger roomed at his home and boarded at his family table with him, his wife and two young children. Mrs. Kreuger's son, Richard, lived with her. She maintained the highest standards of propriety and morality; she constantly manifested great concern for the welfare of her child; and I am convinced that she is an eminently fit and proper person to have custody of her child, Richard."

My ex- told the authorities that my morals were compromised. Some said that Barney had taken both me and Richard away from my ex-husband. We convinced the Reverend Volkert to write a letter affirming me as a fit mother. (The pastor never knew that we had shared a tiny flat over a shoe repair store before we were married.) Rev. Volkert's letter plus my conviction to keep Richard with me finally persuaded the judge to write his verdict.

But my brother William never sent us a sympathy card and refuses to speak to us, especially to his former best friend Barney because he condemns us for loving each other. And Richard's middle name was William in honor of my brother and Barney's good friend.

I must sleep now. It's so hot up here all ready, but a breeze does get up and over the fish market roof into our little window.

Mildred on June 17, 1931

Your Honor: aside from my efforts to run away from reality—I'm a citizen of Lakeshore Bay County, born and raised here. Most of my life was spent here with the exception of eight years spent in the village of Waterloo, Wisc. and surrounding territory as the wife of Richard Kreuger and the mother of Richard Kreuger Jr., born on May 15, 1923 and now deceased. I was married to my first husband on April 2, 1921. A divorce was granted to me on October 16, 1928.

I was educated in the public schools and taught the Christian way of life in Lutheran churches of this city.

This I feel, gives me the right to lay my case before you. You may say this is an unorthodox way of presenting through the church and to come to you as a last resort when these have failed and only court action will relieve the situation. I'm asking you to bear with me, and try to comprehend my dramatic approach to the solution of my problems by trying to realize how one can become dramatic through events over which we have no control.

The fact that I'm a divorced woman should not affect your decisions.

I'm the fifth child of twelve children. When one of us caught some sickness, we would all be quarantined. That one would recover when a second, then a third, fourth and fifth would break out with something and everyone would be quarantined again. I failed in fifth grade at Jefferson School and seventh grade at Martin Luther Christian School, where my mother went to school. I never finished eighth.

My meager education did not stop me from learning as much as I could. I was too young for the older children and too old for the younger ones, so my companions became books. My mother used to swat me whenever she caught me reading instead of doing my chores. But I never stopped my love of books. When I married and moved to Waterloo, I read so much that the librarian ran out of good books for me.

My only other source of education has been through my home and my contacts in trying to be the self-supporting, good citizen we as children are taught to believe every function of government is striving for. My hunger for knowledge is never satisfied.

I went to vocational school for three years while I worked at Farming, Nunn & Busch and the Milwaukee Shoe Factory in Lakeshore Bay. I got an easier job at a candy factory. I've worked as a clerk, a domestic and in a laundry.

I'm now a signwriter and float builder with my husband.

You shall have to go back with me as far as I feel it affects my conscience thinking.

My mother was the oldest of seven children of a good, solid family in this community, people one can be proud to own as a family and would hesitate, except through stress, to besmirch by personal action.

I can't go on. I'm exhausted. Maybe Barney can help finish this.

Mildred on June 20, 1931

Barney. I love him so much but he's not a good provider and I'm too tired to work now.

An Eagle Scout, he's proud of that. Yes, he's trustworthy, loyal and true—but a scout is human too.

He was a guest at a family picnic, the best friend of my brother William. Barney told me that when he looked into my hazel eyes and saw a smile break across my face, he loved me instantly—if I had a husband or not, a son or not, custom be damned—he loved me. I was different, he said, from the women he knew. "I'll always remember," he said, "you skipping through the grass with Richard and how you played and sang and flirted with me across the picnic table." Dick Kreuger wasn't there and I could be myself.

Barney's mother was angry when Barney followed me to California when Junie and I escaped from Waterloo and rode back to Berkeley with Luella. Those roads! We were stranded in a desert town when the car broke down. Luella called her husband, Fred, and he drove for several days to rescue us. Cousins Eugene and my Richard had great fun playing games in the desert while we waited for Fred at the cheap, dusty motel room.

Barney must have missed me or he was envious of my adventures because he decided to hitchhike and ride boxcars across the country with his friend Jack Lange. Well, he claimed his prize when he came to me.

I found love but not security. And now I've lost Richard and I have a newborn on the way.

Jan on September 13, 1972

Had she died from my cesarean birth, I would have been raised by my mother's best friend, Aunt Esther Peterson, part of a congenial extended family of my mother's friends. Esther and her husband were the matron of honor and the best man at my mother's wedding to Richard Kreuger.

I emerged quite free from birth trauma because I missed pushing my way to the light through the birth canal that had been so badly wounded from four illegal abortions during her marriage to Kreuger. Her reproductive system was a mess. Now a wide and jagged cesarean wound inside and outside the gash from her rib cage to her pubic bone had to heal. (I remember when I was ten, I opened her bedroom door to look for her. She was standing naked in front of her full-size mirror. "Look. Look." she said, pointing to that scar. "This is what you did to me.")

Dr. Hanson told my dad he'd done his best during the surgery. A few days later, the doctor said, "You can take her home, but she won't live long."

Mildred didn't die, nor did I.

I lay in isolation. My mouth tastes the pink, fuzzy, hand-me-down blanket wrapped around me. A tired-looking white bunny with black whiskers and a tufted tail decorates it, but that's not enough for me. I root and stubbornly, eagerly look for more. I want softness. I want to be close—and held. My mouth finds the pilling specks of the blanket and the stark coldness of bleached muslin scratching red on my new skin. I feel as if I want to break the binding hold on me and crawl toward my goal, to find what I want. I'm trapped in this blanket that holds me back. It warms me but it restrains me. I'm free from my mother's womb and I'm ready to find her face, her breast, her nourishment, her heartbeat, her arms. Anybody. Somebody. I'm near to her and I think she loves me, but she can't pick me up to draw me close. My lips suck to find her.

My presence was not much comfort to her weakened body and anguished spirit. How would my life have been different if she had died at my birth? My dad would have suffered another disastrous loss: Richard on June 1, 1931, then Mildred at my birth on November 14, 1931, all in less than the two years they were married. Would he have lost me too? Would he have left me, hit the road and ride the rails again? It would be easy to do. To run away. To leave me. Would he have gone looking for adventure and to start a new life?

Emma Schultz Lueckfeld

"Ach do hemmel, du defi asel!"

My mother's parents, Bill and Emma Lueckfeld, argued for decades above the racket of their twelve children, yet, Emma made sure she had spectacular 50th anniversary celebrations in Berkeley, in

Lakeshore Bay where she was born, the locations of her children, her clubs and anywhere else where she could round up a gathering, and she proudly wore her rhinestone tiara.

Bill didn't say much and went along with a glazed look under his bushy eyebrows and a smile plastered below his moustache.

To help make money to raise his large family, Bill would buy run-down houses and repair them for resale. They moved a lot. He ran a saloon on 4th and Wisconsin. Emma baked bread, prepared sausages and meat slices, pickles, potato salad and hard-boiled eggs for the tavern and delivered it all in the baby buggy with her children tumbling along behind.

Emma's oldest child was Arnold, then Eleanora or Ora, Luella, Leona, Catherine, my mother Mildred, William, Elmer, Melvin, Amanda, Emmalynn and finally MayJean. When two or more of them were together, they joked and laughed or quarreled to triumph over each other.

Though most were lucky to finish eighth grade, Mildred and her sisters worked hard to find some fun, an adventure. She told me she would do Egyptian Ella and she danced for me with rigid arms poised in awkward angles, her head undulating on her shoulders. They danced the "Hootchie-Cootchie" and were considered wild by their Lutheran relatives.

Their mother, Emma had a bountiful laugh, but when she was angry, her tongue could chastise the offender faster than any of her twelve kids could run from her. Bill grumbled back at her but he'd heard it all before.

Martin Luther Christian Church, where Emma went to parochial school and her relatives were church elders with a lot of clout forbade Bill from taking communion because he ran that saloon, so they quit the church.

Ora and her boyfriend, "Little Peter" Hansen, told Bill and Emma a lie; that Ora was pregnant so they could get married before she was 16 and free Ora from taking care of all her siblings. When Ora actually did have her baby, she nursed her daughter as well as her youngest sister.

Bold Luella went to California to search for a job. She found a husband for herself and a job for her father who painted trim striping on new Pullman railroad cars. Emma left for Berkeley with five of their youngest kids to join Bill and become an active club woman.

Katherine Rindfleisch Bornofska

"A mighty Fortress is our God,
A trusty Shield and Weapon;
He helps us free from every need
That hath us now o'ertaken...."
The Lutheran Hymnal #262

Though Grandmother Emma wore a sparkling crown at her Golden Anniversary parties, my Grandmother Katie wore something more like a crown of thorns. She was widowed on May 8, 1914, at age 43, after my dad turned ten years old on May 3.

Katherine Rindfleish was born in Lakeshore Bay on February 10, 1871. Henry Bornofska was born in 1858 at the German/Polish borders that shifted with European territorial battles. The family always thought of themselves as German and rejected any reference to Polish origins, even with the "ska" at the end of their name. As the Janes School janitor, he kept the huge building clean and warm. When it snowed, the entire family helped shovel the sidewalk around the entire schoolyard block. With five boys in the family, she maintained a surprisingly calm and orderly household with little excitement or change. My dad had two older brothers and two younger brothers. Every Friday after work, my grandfather would send one of the boys across the backyard to the Douglas Avenue tavern to fetch a pail of beer for him to enjoy. He died after cleaning out the septic tank in the backyard.

Her Lincoln Street home expenses were paid by converting its second story into a rental flat and every cent she gathered went first to pay her mortgage and the real estate taxes so she wouldn't lose her home. I'd watch her roll up a dollar bill or put every coin she could in her sugar bowl on a high shelf over her kitchen table.

Her Anthony, my dad, was a good son and a proud Eagle Scout. He woke early every morning to deliver newspapers in our downtown area, and then he'd go to elementary classes at the First Evangelical Lutheran School. He gave his earnings to his mother.

Henry, her oldest son, was a railroad engineer; Clarence and Elmer were the first movie projectionists in Lakeshore Bay. My father could have gotten jobs through his projectionist brothers—and could earn a decent wage, but he chose to paint signs and be his own boss.

Sometimes I'd climb up the classically grand Venetian balcony stairs and to the smaller Rialto movie houses and watch them with their giant reels of film swirling the projected images below. Sometimes one would give me a nickel and I'd buy sticky, chewy Milk Duds from the lobby vending machine. The youngest son, lean and rugged Roy, bought an old tavern and motel in Manitowish Waters after returning to Wisconsin from California where he and his wife made good money building ships during World War II. Once we visited them up north with Grandma while my dad painted a huge roadside sign for their business. I caught my first musky fish half as long as I was tall with a hook baited with a worm. I pulled it in from the shore but could barely hold it up long enough for a photo.

Seldom would we all gather together as a family, perhaps only at funerals.

Grandma Bornofska befriended me and was kind and patient and though I spent many hours, even months, in her care, I never felt angry or frustrated with her. I'd read a lot. She didn't have a radio. We'd play dominoes. I picked currants, gooseberries and cherries in her yard and ate the jellies, jams and pies she made. Donuts were her specialty, fried on the unevenly heated wood-burning stove. We had to dunk them in milk or milky coffee to bite into them.

When I attended second through eighth grade at Martin Luther Christian School, I'd go to her house three blocks away every weekday and she'd prepare a good lunch for me. I'd run errands for her and in the winter, I'd carry her coal buckets from the basement so that her cooking stove in the kitchen and the pot-bellied stove in her living room would keep her from freezing.

When I was with her on Sunday mornings, she'd take me on the streetcar to her Evangelical Lutheran Church. Except for Christmas Eve or my Confirmation, my parents stayed away from church. I always went alone to my Sunday church services as if those services were another part of going to school. I rode the bus to church and school and everywhere else, I had my wheels of freedom, my boy's bike that I inherited from my cousin.

In winter, Grandma got out of bed early to churn up the coals and hang my clothes on the back of a worn wooden chair to get them toasty for me to jump out of bed and put them on. I'd sleep next to her to keep from freezing. When it was too cold to use the toilet off the kitchen, I peed in her porcelain chamber pot next to the bed and when I finished, I quickly jumped back in her warm bed. The pot was wedged on a shelf under the rungs of the chair with a-just-big-enough hole cut in the seat. A picture on the wall of a gentle, young Jesus stared down at us.

Grandma and I were close but not openly affectionate, yet her home was a safe haven in troubled times. I think I brought some happiness into her life. It was hard to tell because she didn't smile often. One sunny day when I was filled with happy thoughts, I skipped along, thinking of the movie I'd seen, *For Me and My Gal* and a Judy Garland song that my mother and I sang together. "Pack up your troubles in your old kit bag and smile, smile, smile. What's the use of worrying? It never was in style…" I whistled my way up to Grandma's sidewalk, passed her giant, big as a house snowball bush and bounded up the worn steps to her porch and kitchen door. She pointed her finger at me and firmly said, with a slight smile,

"Whistling girls and crowing hens always come to no good ends."

We took care of each other for most of my formative years, but she was tense with my parents. One time I asked my mom why Grandma always calls my dad Anthony, our last name. That's when I learned that he changed his name from Anthony Carl Bornofska to Carl B. Anthony because he wanted to own his own business and "Bornofska" wouldn't work. Perhaps Grandma blamed my mom for that plus made an issue about his choosing a divorced woman for a wife. Dad never said a word against her nor did she say anything negative to me about either of my parents.

When I was older, I realized that my father walked or drove up and down North Main Street within four blocks of her home twice or more each day, but I never knew him to stop for a visit.

Jan from October 10 to 12, 1969

In 1946, a highly respected Lutheran minister who was the father of Faith, my best friend from Martin Luther, tried to recruit me as a student at the new Lutheran High located in the elementary Lutheran school where my father attended years ago.

My mother followed their phone conversation with a letter that I found in her tattered files.

"You are concerned for Jan and others her age who may not live life according to your conception of a Good Way of Life. I shall not send her to the Lutheran High School because God has given us a broad world to live in, and I have every faith that the training she has already received has fitted her with enough knowledge of the laws of the church to make her a good citizen of the world.

"I'm trying to erase a number of critical attitudes which have risen between myself and the church of my people. When Jan confirmed for herself the vows her father and I made for her at baptism, I truly had faith in both God and the child to sever my rule over her soul, except as she may ask me for guidance.

"I have and always will have recognized the good done by the church, but I cannot blind myself to the agony in the world that is caused by it. Jan will naturally be influenced by my attitude. That is where her own relationship between God and herself, in her relationship with the life and death of Christ, will mold her.

"If you have been patient with me to the end of this letter, thank you. I deeply appreciate what Jan's relationship with your daughter and others from the church has done for her.

"That these relationships may be severed, I have no doubt, as that is the way of life, but I'm sure the things she has learned through these associations will influence her in her future actions, good and bad, as much as my own guidance or those of her teachers. She has already taken what each has taught and has weighed them according to her own needs, accepted or rejected them. Any forced influence anyone used from here on is only delaying the beginning of her own life. This I feel we have no right to do. If she is old enough to accept Christ as her savior from original sin, then she is old enough to choose her way of life."

One time my mother came to a parent night and carried on a heated discussion with the minister and the principal. I think that only reinforced the teachers merely tolerating me and sixth through eighth grades were emotionally difficult for me—in addition to what was going on at home.

Like the other girls, I had crushes on boys, and of course, I liked the most popular boy who was an egotistical devil with a foul mouth and a sneaky character. But Kenny was the cutest in the class even though he was one of the shortest. One day he actually spat in my face, for a joke, he said. I hated him, especially after an afterschool club meeting I had at my house.

Many of my friends were distant cousins, offspring of ministers and deacons. They would be angels in front of adults but could be terrors when alone. Our Five Jeeps Club met at different homes and I was proud and happy to be part of this elite, secret "Jeeps" group until we decided to invite some of the boys to visit. My house was the first to hold a boy/girl gathering.

By that time, my father had enlisted in the Navy and my mother waited tables at a nearby luncheonette to make some extra money. There I'd sit on a counter stool and devour a hamburger steak, corn, and mashed potatoes with gravy, maybe sometimes even a piece of their pie. The owner and the regular customers were happy to see me.

Though they seldom went to church, my parents sent me to Martin Luther to get a little religion. It's supposed to be good for everyone. But Martin Luther Christian, I'm afraid, set me against their religion. However, I did get an excellent education in other ways.

I consider myself a rebel during my seven years there. I spoke up for my classmates, defending them against the teachers. I asked questions that challenged the teachers. I don't remember other girls getting sent to the cloakroom or slapped on the hand with a ruler as often.

The boys who misbehaved would get whacked with a rubber hose from teachers' desks. They had to lean with their hands on the teacher's desk, bend over, and get hit on their butts right in front of all of us. When the rubber hose was brought out, we trembled. Some boys got the rubber hose treatment a lot but it didn't seem to cure them. One strong-willed, unrepentant fifth-grader wrestled Mr.

Peters to the floor right in front of the class before help came and before he was whacked with the rubber hose even harder—and longer.

Because the church had German sermons for its parishioners, the students were taught German as well—until World War II. We had Martin Luther's Catechism classes every morning, including memorizing a selected Bible verse every day. I'd practice the verses on the way to school and hoped to be called on last so I'd pick up the words from others' repetition.

Confirmation in 7th and 8th Grades was a big deal. Assistant Pastor Herman taught those classes and unlike our other classrooms with tall windows, this class met in a dark basement room with deeply varnished wainscoting. The desks were in tiers as in a biology lab where students could observe specimens being dissected but science classes had no priority at our school. Evolution and other "heretical" theories defied the "facts" taught to us. God created the earth in seven days 6,000 years ago. Eve, in her second-class status, made friends with a snake, tempting Adam and causing us all to be sinful creatures in constant need of redemption. Jesus died on the cross to save us from sin and rose from the grave on the third day to live again as we would live again in Heaven if we believed in him, and God the Father and the Holy Ghost. You had to promise to be lifelong members of this church forever. Your friends who weren't in our church, especially Catholics and poor pagan souls, would go to hell. And you had to believe all this forever or you would go to hell for eternity.

In addition to these religious concepts, we had to accept a heavy dose of social rules as well.

Dancing is forbidden. Why? Rhythm and movement are natural, like a heartbeat. Playing cards are the work of the Devil. Why? People have fun playing card games—and that includes me. But Jesus had cast the merchants and gamblers out of the temple. You can't join the Boy Scouts or Girl Scouts. Why? I joined the Girl Scouts at a Methodist church for a while and liked it. But "Thou should have no other gods before me." If you go to Girl Scouts, you may as well be Catholic.

Armed with ammunition from my mother's crazy but liberated logic, I chose for myself what was right for me. From my mother's unstable speeches practiced on me, her only audience, and from her reading a quote from Thomas Paine, but I have no idea in what context: "I believe in one God, and no more; and I hope for happiness beyond this life. I believe that religious duties consist in doing justice, loving mercy, and endeavoring to make our fellow-creatures happy. I do not believe in the creed professed by any church that I know of.

Kids would make fun of Pastor Herman, a tall, bulky man in his choking starched collar and stiff black suit and he sweated while trying to control his students. The wrath of God didn't seem convincing coming from this inexperienced pastor who parted his straight hair down the middle of his scalp and used pomade to hold his hair in place. Often, as the class wore on, strands of hair would pop out of the pomade and spring free, rebelling from restraints.

As Confirmation Day grew near Palm Sunday in 1945, I was seriously at odds with myself. How would I stay among my classmates and still conform to these beliefs? These were big issues. I wanted desperately to be a part of the event but I wasn't about to promise—to say yes to these vows.

Oh, I loved Jesus and probably could have vowed to believe in what he represented for all my life, but the other stuff: God the Father who was vengeful and domineering, and the invisible Holy Ghost and Hell and all those Bible myths, and believing everything from only the Bible were not what I could promise to believe, including that the earth was 6,000 years old. What bothered me most was their coercing my classmates and me to promise to be a member all my life—another reason to hold back on affirming any vows on that Palm Sunday.

So I rose and stood with the forty other classmates, all gowned in white robes for the rite of passage of moving from childhood into being adult members of this congregation. The spring sunlight blessed the flowers filling the altar and the two ministers in full pastoral regalia. I stood there and with the deepest respect for my principles and with trust that I'd be understood, even forgiven by the Powers That Be, I stayed silent as my friends, my conforming classmates, answered yes to all the confirmation vows.

That day I took communion for the first and last time—in this Christian tradition. In June, I graduated from the eighth grade and never went back.

One August day, I answered the knock at our side door. It was an unexpected ministerial call from Pastor Herman. I didn't invite him into the house and he never asked to come in. He did ask me where I'd been and we talked for a while in the summer sun, he was on the sidewalk, and I was above him on the porch steps. When he left, no one ever came after me to try to get me to return, to try to save this black sheep so quickly lost from the flock.

I never told my parents that he came, and they never questioned my not going back.

Jan from October 27 to November 23, 1969

Studying my parents' files and typing my findings are emotionally challenging—draining. Combine that with my reporting and feature writing at work, and I'm pressing stationery and carbon paper sandwiches into devouring gluttonous typewriters much of my time. My newspaper stories give me instant gratification. I feel as if I'm accomplishing something useful and important and it moves me beyond the self-pity I could acquire writing about my past. Rather, I'm learning to be more compassionate about my parents and the process is healing.

It's healthy, too, for Alex and me to have several couples circles: high school chums, Alex's work buddies, my older and wiser neighbors Joan Kruse and Adele McEwen, my church friends and Marge Manley.

Alex hates Marge and the time I spend with her because she seems like a liberated and happy divorcee. He never sees how she has to fight with her ex- to get child support. Alex thinks she's a bad example for me and fears I might follow in her footsteps, which makes me furious—as if I don't have a brain of my own nor can I think for myself!

Joan and Adele have imperfect husbands, but they've stayed in their marriages. Once Adele described her husband as a lush and Joan's husband as a genuine alcoholic while she was pouring us another martini. Adele and I commiserate many evenings after supper as we imbibe and laugh together. Matt and Jenny know that if I'm not working on projects in the house, I'm working in the yard or I'm at Adele's kitchen table.

"You know, Adele, I drank my first martini, my first real drink, when I was 18 and my father's date at some American Legion event. We sat at the bar and he asked me what I wanted to drink and I said, "I'll try a drink like that one over there," I pointed, "the one with the olives." Surprised at its taste, I sipped it slowly and with my father at my side, I managed to handle its effects.

Adele, who makes my life look easy and successful, raised five kids with her hard-drinking curmudgeon of a husband. She's older and wiser, caustic yet caring. "Once I asked Ken for money to buy a loaf of bread," she said, "and he gave me exactly thirty-one cents. When Larry was seven, I had to wake him to see if he had a nickel for his brother's lunch money and he said, 'Sure, Mom,' as he rubbed his sleepy eyes, 'How much more do you need.' Another time I didn't speak to Ken for two whole weeks and he never even noticed."

Our kitchen windows are opposite each other and we wave knowingly across her finely manicured yard.

Until my son was 12 and my daughter 10, I allowed my life to be dominated by Better Homes and Gardens expectations. I had no time nor expectations for myself, being totally submerged in others' priorities, including the dog's. Even though I expressed my creativity with my volunteer work, marriage, motherhood and my husband's career defined me.

Alcohol consumption, especially mine, increased dramatically after we moved to South Main Street. One time after drinking and talking with Adele after supper, I staggered through our path between the bushes, stumbled up our front porch steps and struggled to the bedroom. My brain pulse trembled from its center through my body. I lay spread-eagle on our bed and I hung on while the room turned.

Once when Adele and I sat at her kitchen table drinking, I probably complained again about the unhappiness with my marriage. "I'm so bored when I'm with him, but being bored is no grounds for divorce."

She put her elbows on the table and leaned over toward me. "Jan. You and Alex are the perfect couple. Inflation is undermining the economy. Watergate is destroying people's confidence in government. The war in Vietnam is ruining our country's moral fiber. You and Alex and your kids are examples to all who know you that at least the institution of marriage and the family will survive. What will we have to believe in if you and Alex get a divorce?!"

And we poured ourselves another drink.

CHAPTER FIVE

Jan on July 10, 1972

I'm now completing my tenth year of volunteering in various capacities, several or all of them at the same time as a church school teacher, superintendent, chair and member of the RE committee and I've succeeded in my final goal of having the church board hire Marge Manley as the first paid RE director, even if it's only a small stipend.

Marge's appointment and the annual RE Day service with Anna, Marge and me was the culmination of a successful year, except for one fight with Alex after I made a rousing speech at our church's annual meeting. I dared to ask him what he thought about my presentation while he was driving home.

"You're doing too much being away from the family. That's where your focus should be, especially when I have to take so many out-of-town business trips. You need to take care of the children and our home."

We pulled into our driveway and I walked ahead of him. Again, no positive response from him—merely tolerance or negative feelings that could last for days. I was beginning to learn new words from my secret feminist readings: "the loss of self-esteem" and "patriarchy."

Matriarchy vs. patriarchy? No. I didn't want power over others; I wanted equality. I also wanted confirmation of my worth from those I care for and some freedom from the restraints that frustrated my need to grow toward personal goals. But I also wanted my children.

When we're at home, I'm the mother of his children who makes the most of our marriage relationship. I became an actor playing the wifely role of a subordinate who looks in the mirror of her life and sees surrender and resignation. The continuing lack of equality with him on personal and significant issues caused me to think that my husband was becoming incredibly dull. He was unhappy with me because I was working and involved in feminist awareness as if he thought, "She'll get a taste of freedom and never come back."

One day I actually surveyed the newsroom, thinking about having an affair with one of the men I work with, looking for someone to love and to love me. I was so lonely, empty and abjectly bored with my husband. My children were nine and eleven; otherwise, I may have filed for a divorce. But I had "everything a woman would want" and didn't think that boredom and other emotional malaise could be legal grounds for divorce. And the available men I considered for an affair were worse than Alex, so what would I have gained?

My only bright lights are my children plus the successful Montessori school and RE program, yet during that era, I was homebound. He allowed me, yes, he allowed me to attend a Montessori board meeting and chair a RE committee night each month and if I went out without him more than that, he'd grumble passively about the values of home and family. And now I'm writing exciting articles for the newspaper. I realized that the more I accomplished get, the more passive he becomes, except in bed, and I was getting angrier and angrier inside.

That last RE speech incident gave me a perverse idea. Adele McEwen worried about her daughter Liz, who had newly graduated from college and living in Boston. I offered to drive Adele to Boston to see her. Adele loved the idea, but she couldn't help drive and we didn't want me to do it all. That's when I checked with Marge, whose income depended on her ex's uneven child support checks and she needed an inexpensive vacation from her boys before starting her RE responsibilities.

Because of his devotion to Adele, Alex grudgingly let us use the station wagon and the three of us headed east, feeling free, anticipating adventures.

We put Adele in charge of the money and Marge and I drove. I did the driving, even in Boston and felt my adrenalin pumping and being exhilarated when I made all the right moves on the one-way maze of crowded streets with insane drivers. We met with Elizabeth, and visited what we called the UU Vatican at 25 Beacon Street and other famous UU people and our country's literary and religious historic places.

One day Adele, Liz and her boyfriend took a trip to Rockport and Marge and I ventured together in a similar direction and enjoyed a most memorable lunch of fried clams near Rockport. It wasn't the clams that impressed me, it was sitting across the table at our oceanside window with the sun warming us as we exchanged intimate, heartfelt thoughts about our lives. Then Marge and I walked south along the shore and onto a lane surrounded by a large cluster of beach bushes and trees. We were astounded when we met Adele and her entourage walking toward us from the north along the same path. The surprise, laughter and celebration of this phenomenon set the carefree mood for the entire trip—as if it all were meant to be.

"New York! New York! What a wonderful town."

Marge made hotel arrangements through her ex's New York City resident relatives who had many connections, including show business people. Following her directions into Manhattan, we discovered our black station wagon snarled in the midst of garishly decorated cars with drinking drivers weaving their way to the city's festive and spicy Latin-American Day parade. Then I was astounded when we pulled up to a posh hotel on 7th Avenue across from Carnegie Hall. After helping us with our luggage, a valet kidnapped the car and we checked into our plain but adequate suite. Impossible! Someone made a mistake! We can't afford this! And after checking reception before we unpacked, our reservation was indeed correct for a price that we could afford.

After cocktails in our suite before we were to head for supper, my happiness level spiraled. I was in accommodations on The Great White Way off Times Square with my friends together in the Big Apple. We chose a nearby French restaurant and I danced, crossing the street and spinning around signposts. Adele told me to calm down. Marge took me by the arm.

The next day we toured the city, the museums, the shops. "The Bronx is up and the Battery's down." I bought a sterling silver ballpoint pen at Tiffany's. We visited Marge's ex's aunts in their tastefully decorated apartment and enjoyed their hospitality and stories of life in the city. I was in awe of being with people who lived a life that I would have wanted to try.

After bailing our car out of valet parking the next morning, I aimed it toward Times Square with confidence and pride and maneuvered it perfectly through the greatest intersection in the world toward the Lincoln Tunnel, New Jersey and along highways that took us home. We were new women after our adventure. Adele was assured that her daughter was safe. We three met new people, visited exciting places and were independent women—at least for a while.

After the trip was over, Adele admitted to me that she didn't like Marge, who pushed her a bit too far during the long hours of the drive home about trying to rekindle Adele's sex life.

But Marge captivated me and became more like a sister, my best friend, which made Alex dislike her even more.

I searched for solutions to my frustrations and nurtured new dimensions in my life by journaling, reading and selecting music and movies to broaden my understanding. One morning months later, I woke up and gave myself permission to love others beyond my family and I realized that I didn't have to restrict my love to men. I became open to new emotions and found myself having deep and intense feelings for Marge.

I drove my kids nuts with my obsessive playing of Cat Steven's *Tea for the Tillerman* album and the song asking, "How can I tell you that I love you? I love you/But I can't think of right words to say."

After folk dancing on Friday night with my children and our friends, I wrote in my journal on Saturday:

"It was an August morning when I burst out of bed to the window toward the lake and became a new person. The rising sun sparked silver rays across smooth water toward me and I felt its energy. I realized that I was in love and I gave myself permission to explore the depths of this incredible feeling. An exhilarating, breathtaking, joyful secret—I love. I give love. I am ready to share my love."

I was careful not to wake my sleeping husband and break the glorious mood and the vibrating tension of my newfound emotion that may be broken by the pragmatic evaluation he makes of me.

Inspiration

A life is lit from many sources
that radiate warmth and light.
Uncounted stars shine on solemn emptiness.
Clusters of crystals add sparkle
that brighten a cool, cloudless night
and lights the way to infinity.

A vast darkness is penetrated
by ribboned rays from the moon,
slender illusions of warmth,
cool and blue, uncommitted in space,
pulling at tides, at hearts, at lunatics
who need to be moved in the night.

The sun's light is too huge to be seen.
Its warmth is felt beyond horizons,
melting white ice, making life new,
 pulling green and good from the earth.
Yet stand too long in its radiance,
 the distant heat will sear and scar.

In contrast, is the seething lava
 within the aching gut,
 or the brilliant flame within the soul of one
 who stands in awe— defenseless, by choice,
while absorbing life's lights
from whatever the source.

Jan in May 1971

I made elaborate plans to show Marge my poem and tell her how I felt about her. For days I drove for miles looking for the perfect, private, comfortable place to be with her, with champagne, a picnic supper and all. I even considered walking out to the end of the Lake's protecting breakwater across from my house, but her legs would be too short to hop across the rocks and she'd be too tired to pay attention to me.

Her sons were away so we ended up in her quiet and calm living room where we could talk without interruption. Scared and excited, choking so I wouldn't cry, I told her that I had fallen in love with her. It was the most nerve-wracking, body-trembling encounter I'd ever experienced. I could barely breathe.

I handed her my poem and explained, "In my 'Inspiration,' the second stanza is about Alex, and the third is about you, Marge. The last, of course, is about me."

She was exceptionally cool yet understanding, but she couldn't, she said, return that kind of love. That was okay for me in my panicky mode because I didn't know what I'd do next. But if I'd been a man, she would have taken me by the hand and bedded me in a minute. She kindly acknowledged my feelings but never returned them at any emotional intensity.

We continue to be close friends and do a lot together, but I wouldn't get too close to her. I would love her, write her poems, entertain her and cater to her wishes, but without any overt physical contact. And I love her mother and her sons.

I devised reasons for Marge and me to be together. I planned my first all-women's Door County weekend in June and invited five of my best UU friends, more than enough to fill up our little trailer: Diana Dixon, Betty McGregor, Anna and Marge. Diana said Nick had asked her why she wanted to go off with that bunch of lesbians.

I made a bed on the trailer's collapsible table for Betty and Diana to sleep on its upholstered cushions. Rather than sleep close to Betty, Diana put an air mattress on the narrow floor. She later switched herself around so she wouldn't breathe any bottled gas fumes from the little furnace vent.

Anna slept in the upper bunk inches under the ceiling and I worked it out to sleep with Marge in the lower berth. I was so intensely in love with her that I couldn't sleep while I lay as close to her as possible without ever touching her—ever. I lay awake all night, overcome with joy and ecstasy, listening to her, feeling her body heat within the sleeping bags I had zipped together—for extra warmth, I explained.

I cooked for them what I had prepared at home. One milk carton was to be a hardy soup, but I discovered it to be frozen turnips and other root veggies. Before cocktail time, I drove to our only store, bought and added some spicy sliced brats and horseradish sauce for my brew and it became almost gourmet. We sang and folk danced in our field, toured and stopped at many little shops. Anna bought a tole blue enamel ladle for me in recognition of being "The Soup Queen." We went up to see Diana's The Big Forty, ate a Door County fish boil one night, repaired a faulty car part and returned home feeling liberated.

I was exhausted yet exhilarated.

Jan on August 25, 1972

How could folk dancing be a hostile act? The McGregor's taught Anne, Marge, other friends, children, teens and elders to folk dance in our church's cramped Sunday school church basement. We'd dance the grapevine, detouring around posts, holding hands in a line and feeling the rhythmic soul of the international folk music vibrate through us.

I'd always been thrilled by off-pitch beats of Armenian music played for hours at their annual church picnics, but I didn't dance because Alex didn't want to, or because I was pregnant, or chasing after Matt and Jenny, even Sona when she was a toddler. I didn't want to look foolish either because I was one of the few "odars" or non-Armenians among them. Slow dances were Alex's choice. In high school, he would quietly come from behind me among my crowd of girlfriends after I had led one of them around the floor in jazzy jitterbugging and he would tap me cautiously on the shoulder, his cue to ask me to shuffle a close two-step when the music slowed down just in time to ask to walk me home.

Our folk dance group soon grew in numbers enough to qualify for using the community center on Friday nights. Often dancers would invite young and old to their homes for refreshments after the dance.

But Friday night was also couples mixed tennis at the indoor racquet club where Alex and I played a mean game together against all comers. Though I truly enjoyed playing tennis, I missed dancing and when Matt and Jenny were old enough to come with me, I ached to dance—and go to the parties afterward with my kids and dancers of all ages.

Alex refused to come with us, to even compromise and take turns between Friday night tennis and folk dancing. A simple question without an answer: What would have happened in my life if Alex had joined us in folk dancing?

Alex and I would go to plays and movies. *Slaughterhouse-Five* from Kurt Vonnegut's book, resonated with us both especially learning about the firebombing of Dresden that killed as many people as the atom bombs in Japan. We lived in Frankfurt in West Germany for two-and-a-half years, but none of our American friends and colleagues knew or spoke of that because the Army's *Stars & Stripes* media didn't cover that disaster that was in the Russian sector. Of course, we didn't speak much about the Holocaust, either. We just traveled about eating delicious cuisine and hitting the jazz spots, truly enjoying ourselves when Alex's Signal Corps and my teaching at the Army dependents' high school didn't interfere with our good times. *Slaughterhouse-Five* filled in far-out information and fantasy for us in swiftly shifting time and settings. Billy Pilgrim innocently wandered about from real to imagined worlds. Can imagine worlds become real? Whatever. Alex's new expression now is Billy Pilgrim's favorite, "And so it goes."

And so it does go. He finally did his own thing on Friday night and I did mine, especially when I wanted to spend as much time with Marge as I could. He could also see how pleased I was with her and how I desired to be with her. He hated her, "She was a bad influence, being divorced and all, whatever!" And what does "all" mean?

He was never happy about our church parties or any other social gathering unless it was strictly couples, where he expected me to be at his elbow catering to him or being responsible for maintaining our part of conversations.

A few of our UU social activities for me became the closest scene in the Midwest to California hippiedom. We UU adults had a "hippie" overnight at the church. I went alone and drank too much homemade wine. Bob McGregor drove me home early that morning as sick as I could be, pale and shaky. I staggered straight to bed and for hours, Alex scraped wallpaper off the wall next to our bedroom where I was trying to sleep. At about 4 p.m., I phoned to ask my hard-drinking neighbor Adele for some sympathy and asked her what to take or do for a cure.

She said, "Well, Jan, it's almost cocktail hour."

Once Alex and I went in togas to a Roman orgy organized by a UU friend for her professor husband's fortieth birthday party. Marge and I pooled our play money and aggressively bought male "slaves" at the auction and had them give us soothing massages. My massages were mild with Alex keeping a close eye on me. I don't even know if he let himself be part of the auction. Besides, I wasn't interested in owning male slaves, only sharing them with Marge.

"I was surprised that the orgy actually turned out to be one," said our hostess. "There'll be Mazola salad oil marks on the rugs forever."

Jerry and Joyce Shannon's home had a path down the lake bank to the brisk Lake Michigan waters. Their house was equipped with a sauna, hot tub, and ping pong table, plus their playful attitude that encouraged all concerned. He would take his turn hosting folk dancing parties, as did I at our house, but his house had more toys.

The Shannons also invited us to an annual sauna, skinny-dipping, and brass quartet concert between Christmas and New Year. Of course, Alex shied away from that party too.

CHAPTER SIX

Bea on June 24, 1972

I hope no one finds a couple of stories I've stashed away in my bedroom until I'm dead.

When I was about eight, I got the beating of my life.

My supposedly good friend Mary Lou came roaring home to my mother to tattle on me. I was ensconced in an apartment vestibule with two other girls, including one named DoDo. They dared me to lick DoDo's cunt and I was in the process of experimenting with that endeavor when Mary Lou ratted on me and my mother called me home.

"What were you doing!?" Mother demanded.

"Nothing," I replied. Wherewithal, my mother grabbed me by one hand and walloped me with the other, going round and round the room as I yowled in protest. Truth be told, I had no idea what my mother was so upset about.

This whole adult sex thing is so confusing. What the hell do they want anyway?

I always seemed to chum in triads in my life. Teenagers Hannah and Lois and I started going to the Midwest Bible Church with its talk of sin and being saved. I'm quite sure that I'd sinned up 'til now. No one can tell me why, but there's always lurking in my mind about something being funny about that episode with DoDo in the apartment vestibule.

We became involved with Youth For Christ and traveled downtown to the Moody Bible Institute to hear Billy Graham preach.

I was so moved I walked down the aisle.

"She is SAVED!" I heard and was taken backstage and prayed with and they gave me Bible verses and I was redeemed. Now I will go to Heaven!

Later I returned to a giant Youth For Christ Rally broadcast on the radio with thousands of people and God knows how many listeners in the radio audience. I was selected to give my testimony on the radio and I told thousands how I was a sinner and now I am saved.

As a Pioneer Girl with Hannah and Lois, we fell in love with our leader, hanging around her house to bill and coo whenever she gave us the least bit of attention. But Hannah and Lois did not go to Camp Ojibwe as I did at 14 after eighth-grade graduation when my mother made me a lovely white dress. But alas, I didn't fill out the top quite to her expectations, so Mother bought me a padded bra to wear that day. I only wanted a pair of leather lace-up, high-top boots. After graduation Mother bought me the coveted pair that I took on my first excursion to the Christian Camp Ojibwe.

What fun. I went camping for two weeks for two years.

In the second-year at 15, I had the best time. I discovered kissing. Other girls also had and we'd practiced these arts at all times at camp: in the tent, on the pathways and especially in front of the mess hall before meals. My special friend was Lou and we'd kiss and kiss and enjoy ourselves immensely. No one told us there was anything wrong with this activity.

We kept in touch by phone after camp, calling each other "husband" and "wife" and when my mother overheard us, she spouted, "Don't say that!" But alas, she never told me why I shouldn't and I remained eternally confused.

Surprise! When I was 16, I was invited to be on the boys' camp staff at Camp Ojibwe for the whole summer in exchange for room and board! That summer, I discovered boys. I met Fred and experimented with boy-girl kissing, which was as much fun as last year. Unfortunately, at Camp Court, I was tried for "robbing the cradle." Fred was eight months younger than I. Both of us were disgraced and thrown off the pier into the lake. I was also told that I wouldn't be on the staff during the girls' camp, which comes for two weeks at the end of the season. This is what I'd been waiting for so I opted to attend anyway—as a camper.

It took me a long time to figure this whole thing out, but finally, it dawned on me that they hired me to work at the boys' camp because they thought I was queer and wouldn't get involved with the boys and they had already made up their minds that I wouldn't be allowed to contaminate the girls during girls' camp.

I don't forgive them for this. Nor do I forgive my mother for not standing by me. Instead, she forced me to go to work in a factory to pay back the money for the girls' camp that I'd opted to attend.

While playing clarinet in the high school band for two years, I switched to the viola and the orchestra and new vistas suddenly opened up for me. I formed a new triad relationship with Liv and Gloria.

But it's Liv that I fell madly in love with. Liv became my best friend and mentor and a deep bond formed between us, a wholesome relationship filled with deep emotional and intellectual respect.

Jan in Door County on August 24, 1972

In the few quiet moments that I have, when I'm too tired or too tense to evaluate objectively or with resignation my job as mother/wife, I think of my friend Marge, my comparatively free spirit. My friend already has two sons of her own with ages farther apart than mine.

How I would love for us to share more of what we are and what we have. I think in ideals—of sharing our beautiful and happy, compatible children, our magnificent Door County space, our mutual interests. Sisters can do this, if they survive sisterhood. What about soul sisters? What about friends?

Yet what I cherish is tempered and conditioned by cruel logic and a desperate realization that what I am and what I have are not my own to freely share.

Still, in the peaceful moments that I have, I think of my friend—a comparatively free spirit.

To Whom It May Concern,

Because my will is jointly written with my husband and because I do not have time now to express any separate wishes in legal documents, I would like informally to express my hope that if both my husband and I die before our two children reach the age of majority, I hope that someone from the circle of my good friends at the Unitarian Universalist Church friends (like Marge Manley or Anna Spence) would ask the court for guardianship of our children. These persons or this person may or may not be a couple. We have friends who are married and who would make excellent foster parents for my children, but we also have friends without marriage partners who would also make an excellent home and parent for them.

I would also restate our wishes expressed in my will that no member of either my or my husband's family be chosen as guardian for our children. Though we love and care for our relatives, each of them has inherited, acquired and passed on a lifestyle of unhappiness and negativism. My church family members share their joy and their light; they are strong in their love and tender in their understanding and my children love many of them as much as I do.

Respectfully
Jan D. Carnigian

My Matt and Jenny are great kids. I trust them to be responsible and independent and they are. They spend much of their time with our UU and folk dancing teenagers and Matt tolerates Jenny, the youngest of the group, to tag along. My part-time jobs are close and I'm available whenever and if they need me. My editor knows where I am on assignment or my hospital can page when I'm out of my office.

We've all had fun furnishing our barn and enjoying the land and the area. Jenny and I do a lot of reading while the boys go fishing.

When I'm without Alex, I can read my *Ms. Magazines* that I must otherwise hide because he gets sullen when he sees me reading them. I'm also reading Sylvia Plath's autobiographical novel, *The Bell Jar,* Nena and George O'Neill's *Open Marriage* which jolts readers when they realize there are options to traditional marriage models and Eric Berne's *The Games People Play* about transactional analysis (TA) and understanding human behavior.

Recently, I started reading Nigel Nicolson's *Portrait of a Marriage*, a description of the loving open and bisexual marriage of his father, Harold Nicolson and Nigel's mother, Vita Sackville-West, all of London's multi-talented and brainy Bloomsbury Group rebels.

Her son found his mother's diary describing her loving women and based this book on that. He failed to note that his father too was bisexual and that the couple loved each other even when they had many liaisons outside of their marriage. Vita had several women lovers and she even ran away to Europe with one, dressing sometimes as a man and thoroughly enjoying that gender's freedom. She and Virginia Woolf were tender friends and lovers until Woolf, terrified of going mad again, committed suicide by drowning herself in the Ouse River.

How could I even entertain thoughts that Alex would understand my love for a woman and still let me keep my home, family and him? Dreams. Foolish dreams. Stupid dreams. And what about society? We, especially he, certainly aren't candidates for open marriage nor are we England's Bloomsbury group of free-loving intellectuals. And Sylvia Plath is almost more famous for killing herself than she is for her poems and writing.

Jan on October 28, 1972

Work at the newspaper is progressing with my holiday and human interest stories and then there are always weddings and fifty-year wedding anniversary announcements that are so tedious, and you have to be careful you leave nothing out, or your women's editor will get complaints. Wedding rituals with mothers' hand-sewn beaded gowns and flowing veils make me think of ancient ceremonies preparing virgins for the sacrifice.

I did interject Hanukkah among holiday assignments. So many people, even newspaper editors, take it for granted that everyone's Christian.

My city editor assigned me to cover this AA speaker. I didn't know what I was getting into. I'd passed this AA building hundreds of times but I never thought I'd be going there. I took Alex with me, introduced ourselves to the speaker, and proceeded to take notes.

"Nun Frankly Describes Her Days as Former Alcoholic"

by Jan Carnigian

When a Catholic nun, wearing her religious, though modern habit, spoke frankly of her experiences as an alcoholic to 80 persons at the monthly open meeting of the Alano Club, she gave hope and reassurance to other alcoholics who share this problem.

She revealed the details of her life as a victim of alcoholism and the changes in her life since she because active in Alcoholics Anonymous.

She said, "When I realized I was an alcoholic first and a sister second, then I was able to face my problem and work to solve it."

A first-grade teaching nun for 34 years, she'd lived with guilt, remorse, and fear, thinking that if a sister could be an alcoholic and be discovered by others as one, people would think, "What is the church coming to?"

"As if I were the church," she said in a humble tone.

"For those many years, I thought I was more than human, but now I realize I'm only human with all the faults and foibles of a human being."

Her one desire is to help another sister overcome the disease of alcoholism. "God gave me this disease for a reason." With recent changes in the Catholic Church, and greater freedom in the lives of sisters, she said they would have many more temptations to overcome.

She discovered last week that in her community of 700 sisters that covers an area from the east coast to Nebraska, 22 nuns are in need of alcoholic counseling.

Living in Chicago, she is active in the Mustard Seed Group, an Alcoholic Anonymous organization. She even visits Skid Row areas where the men there recognize her as an alcoholic though she wears her nun's habit.

"I'm grateful to Almighty God and the AA program, which is the Lost and Found Department. Thank God I'm found again."

The sister was raised in a family of 12 where alcohol of all types was in the home, and her parents tried teaching its use in moderation. She said she became the only family member who became a member of a religious order—the only one who became an alcoholic.

"In our home, my brothers and sisters could have fun and drink and then stop, but I'd continue to drink, even sneaking more when no one was looking," she revealed.

"If we only knew what a cunning, insidious, and progressive disease this is and what it can do to us when we begin...." she reflected.

When she entered the convent to become a nun, there were strict controls and her alcoholism didn't affect her for three years.

But when she became a teaching sister, her preoccupation with alcohol and the loss of control over its consumption began. She was able to keep it under control during the teaching week, she said but not on the weekends.

She revealed the fears of being discovered, the attempts to hide her drinking, and her desperate loneliness because of these fears and hiding. "There were times when I hid several Four Roses bottles under my habit, hoping that they wouldn't clink together, full or empty, under my rosary to betray my duplicity. I've been to hell and back and never want to go back in that cage again," she stressed. "How Almighty God put up with me, I'll never know."

She never missed a day of school from drinking or from any other sickness, she said, and then she joked, "With all that anti-freeze in me, how could I catch a cold?"

She described different methods of getting alcohol and hiding it or the empty bottles in the convent. Because she had a large family, she asked for and received gifts of money or alcohol "...for occasional parties for the sisters, I'd tell them individually, and then drink it all myself." Then she would suffer the guilt of her duplicity in addition to the remorse of her drinking.

In her 34 years of teaching, she has been transferred to 15 of the 38 missions in her order and spent each summer in the motherhouse…under close supervision of her superiors, "…who protected and shielded me, but they had no idea what a sick alcoholic was and they had never heard of treatment centers or of Alcoholics Anonymous. No one ever dreamed that a sister could be an alcoholic."

One transfer sent her to a convent in Chicago that housed over 20 sisters. As in the past, she started her new assignments with the best intentions not to start drinking again. "But one hot day, I was sent to the storage room with a key to put some soda in the refrigerator. Then I opened the door, I found a case of beer and that was all I needed to begin again."

The beer and liquor found there were for the use of the 20 sisters, and the janitor would replace any that was used, she explained. "But I was the only one who drank any."

After that year in Chicago, which she described in frank detail as the worst time of her life, she was transferred to Kentucky, "…of all places," she said, "where I quickly discovered many sources of supply in those mountains."

Finally, her superiors told her that if she did not control her drinking, she would not be able to teach again. They had made arrangements to send her to an alcoholic treatment center in Hazelton, Minnesota. Her first thought was if she would have to wear her nun's habit and if another nun had ever been there before.

"My pride was as great as my embarrassment, and I was afraid. As in the past, I would start worrying about what would happen to me, start drinking, and then feel guilt and remorse for drinking."

Her loneliness was intense at the center because she feared everyone would judge her as a nun even though she was wearing lay clothes supplied for her there. She attended all the classes and acknowledged the special help given to her by the staff, but because she continued to isolate herself from the other patients, she failed to be helped until someone said behind her back, "Yes, that's the nun."

With all pretexts gone, she was then able to unburden herself, make friends with other alcoholics, and share the experiences, strength, and hopes to overcome the disease.

Her following association with members of AA, being accepted and cared for by fellow alcoholics, made her realize on her way to recovery that the loneliness she once knew needed never be again.

"The love and devotion shown to me by the prayerful life of my fellow AA members have added more to my spiritual life than even my life in the convent because these people care for each other and realize the value in other human beings."

As a reporter interested in the human potential movement, I asked to be assigned to cover a weekend Transactional Analysis (TA, I'm OK, You're OK) in Lakeshore led by a psychologist from Milwaukee. Another motive was to introduce the material to the community. Our RE committee meetings discussed offering a TA weekend retreat at our church. Dawn introduced me to Rachael Sandler as our possible TA workshop leader. Marge, Anna and I went to one of her Saturday sessions in her home, underwent some insightful experiences in her group and we invited her to lead two weekend sessions for next year's adult RE programming.

I'd been given some controversial reporting assignments lately with my editor's growing awareness of our similar political leanings. Then we became ecology-oriented and printed green and white Whole Earth flag logos and global warming stories. Even if my stories were factual and unbiased, several of us liberals would share our opinions. My recent assignments included "Readers Express Views on Abortion Controversy" and "UW Students Picket School."

As a reporter as well as a member of Another Mother for Peace, I was assigned a story, "A Palestinian Views the Near East." My lead quoted the Palestinian saying, "You never know what will happen to you when you travel through Arabian countries. You can be riding in a car with a person who looks suspicious to the authorities and you may spend a month in jail or you can be killed—shot at the border."

After vandals spilled blood on Lakeshore Bay's Army draft files, a vague, unsigned letter addressed to me at work could have been from one of them. I showed it to John and after reading it, he took the letter and the envelope and put his fingerprints all over the paper and envelope. I took a turn adding my fingerprints as well. He reported the letter to the authorities and that afternoon, the police photographed and fingerprinted both of us. Nothing else happened to us or to the original vandals.

"Nudity Ordinance Resumes Thursday"

"By Jan Carnigian" was branded across the front page in bold headlines—with my by-line. The media was called at eight a.m. to meet with the mayor, who condemned the meddling press and berated us for printing the leak about a conflict in the laws controlling nude dancers and massage parlors. Curiously I had to look up the usage of 'erogenous zones' as a term to avoid printing all the specific erotic specifications listed in the proposed city ordinance. I must admit that it titillated my journalistic skills. Lakeshore Bay's ordinance banned nudity "and other Bacchanalian revelries" in local cabarets and listed several regulations for owners and entertainers, including "Costumes will be of sufficient, non-transparent material to cover the upper and lower erotic zones."

My inclusion of the words "areola having to be covered" was edited out.

Later at home, Alex commented, "I see your story made the front page."

As an outspoken feminist, I was assigned to cover Norman Mailer's visit to UW-Oshkosh. Perhaps my colleagues thought I'd get into a verbal scrap with him.

"Norman Mailer Uses Verbal Overkill to Assault Adversaries"

By Jan Carnigian

I wrote: Norman Mailer, the tiger of the new journalism and violator of women's liberation, is a big pussycat.

Scratch him behind his ears through his silver steel-woolly curls. He may roll over and purr, but he's never off balance for long. And he does have claws.

Mailer is still the Jewish boy from Brooklyn who shouts obscenities to get your attention. But if you don't lose your cool, keep your sense of humor and pay him some mind, he can reach through your prejudices and make you think and feel.

In his singular line of logic, he makes gross statements about the failure of vaginal orgasm that follows on to the incapacity of "the American Will" to admit to problems it cannot solve, especially the war in Vietnam.

"The Evening with Norman Mailer" could have been a verbal boxing event as Mailer challenged all comers to take issue with him. He entered the vastness of the field house, walking with a boxer's gait, to plant himself firmly in place in front of the bleacher-seated audience. You could visualize a terry-clothed gym towel draped over his blue blazer as he confidently entered the arena. The gymnastic equipment, parallel bars, rings and balance beam stored behind him added to the image.

The only battlers willing to take on the self-proclaimed literary champion of the world were a couple of women.

They seemed eager, poised to pounce on the alleged arch-male chauvinist. With a whimsical glint in his eye that said he had hooked a live one, Mailer dispatched his vulnerable victims by badmouthing their logic along with their posteriors.

In his conflict with women liberationists, Mailer seems to be winning battles while he's losing the war.

During a press conference later that evening, I asked Mailer why he was so hostile, especially about women. "Many things you say reveal to many so much integrity and importance, why do you alienate the very people who would support your political opinions?"

He answered that he was against totalitarianism of any kind, including militant woman's lib advocates, but that he wouldn't go out for any block support. He spoke of the complexities of the issues, yet he said that women must admit to some dichotomies in life that pertain to the separate functioning of the sexes.

And he admits to having made "a few foolish remarks when I was in a peevish mood" that has been criticized by militant women.

After knocking Women's Lib out in the first round, Mailer got to the main event, the American political scene, including the war and the "Mind of the Wad."

Mailer challenged "objectivity." He does not accept the concept of "fact."

Passing as an Aquarius, Mailer writes about news events in the third person and adds his presence to what he sees. Nixon advocates probably wouldn't even read or come to hear Mailer, unless they, like the radical women's lib people and some masochists, enjoy being wiped out by verbal overkill.

As Aquarius describes a worship service for Republicans, he wrote that they were praising the heart of God in orderly America. With the war, they could not see, "the war is high in the sky, goodness was there in the field of America—But the fear of fire was beneath."

To further illustrate the contrast in the good, clean personality of the Republican Party, he read about the man who would take a walk each night and defecate on the lawn of a stranger. Each night this would happen and finally, when the man was forced to stop and was taken away, he screamed, "I need to (common word for bowel movement) on that lawn to keep my body in shape."

He told his youthful audience of about 1,000 how to counter the effects of the "damp, dull wad of America."

He said, "Know what you think, learn how to know what you think and have new thoughts—move like a river."

He would remake society to have the masses educate themselves. "Stupidity is a choice." And he would remove obstacles to the education of the electorate. "Parts of the body are never used and mass man has never used his wits," he said.

If you acknowledge Mailer's concept of "personal journalism" by returning the smile and if your tactics are not hostile, the tiger of the new journalism and the violator of women's liberation is a big pussycat."

I was so proud of what I had accomplished and so were my colleagues. But when I returned to my desk the next day, I found a handwritten note saying, "Great work, Jan. But Shit! Don't you know that 'deficate' is spelled with an 'e'?"

Alex commented, "I thought your story on Norman Mailer would be longer."

Faint praise and indifference were his weapons rather than affirmation. Later, I watched a TV version of Ibsen's play *The Doll's House* and wept when I heard Nora say, "I want to be understood and I want to be understood by someone who wants to understand me and who needs it for himself. I have water in my veins, colored water and the color I've borrowed from you. What I want is blood—my own blood."

CHAPTER SEVEN

Jan on March 10, 1973

In January, I started organizing what I've hidden away for a long time: my past writing and collections of articles, favorite song lyrics like The Beatles' "Eleanor Rigby" and "In My Life" with favorite poems, quotes from plays that touched me, nighttime scribblings in my notebook on my bedside table, whatever. My mother's worn portable Smith Corona typewriter gets a good workout in my studio in our fourth bedroom.

After a long absence, Bea Lindberg reappeared now as a frail and slender femme fatale with long, dark brown hair centered by striking, wispy streaks of gray cascading down, framing her face and curling at her shoulders into the subtle crevices of her collarbone. She wears tight, black body shirts that also reveal the soft rise of her breasts made more prominent in contrast with her slight body. Artistically applied make-up with blue eye shadow and black liner accent the emotionally charged person within her new image.

Vulnerable yet svelte in her flared-cuffed pants covering her mid high-heeled boots, she drapes her upper hipline with silver belts or sashes. Old friends don't recognize her at first. It's Bea, seething with sexuality, especially when she assumes the pose of putting her hands on her cocked hips to imitate her heroine Diana Rigg as Emma Peel in TV's *The Avengers*.

The first time she came into my life in 1962 with four kids in tow, her matronly form projected solid determination, her brown eyes, alert skepticism. This time her stunning transformation indicates how brittle she is, and her brown eyes reveal how apprehensive she is as she watches her own world evolving.

Being a curious listener of her intriguing stories mixed with sardonic comic touches, I found out that her teenagers are driving her wild. She's having a lot of fun with them, composing stories and songs, singing and playing the piano, and learning to play the guitar with them, but they're all at her house almost around the clock, even when school is in session because her kids' friends who don't go to school keep coming over during the day.

The kids collected money recently for a surprise wedding anniversary party for "Mrs. L." and "Poor Pop Jake." They bought them a new couch because the teens wore out the old one. One of the young guys, who actually moved into their little house for three weeks, got a crush on irresistible Bea with her new look. He wanted to dance with her when they were alone and hinted about having further privileges. She told me she straightened him up in a hurry and sent him back to his parents' home.

Bea's father keeps getting sick enough to go to hospitals and nursing homes, where she visits him every day. When she was told he'd be in nursing homes for life, that his brains were fried, her father gave her power of attorney and she sold his house.

Bea still doesn't have a full-time professional teaching position and her unsolicited manuscript submissions keep coming back rejected. She's losing interest in her writing groups, her art classes, and in her boring husband even though she tries to join in some UU couples' gatherings in Southport and with friends Angie and Steve Murak, their neighbors when their kids were small.

Bea told me that she decided that she needed to go back to the Unitarian Universalist Church— this time not for her kids but for herself—to meet with her UU friends who are her intellectual equals. I convinced Bea to come folk dancing with her old friends, the McGregor's, Anna Spence, Marge Manley, our kids and me. "It will be so good for you," I said. "You don't need a partner to join in the line, and we often get together afterward and party at someone's home."

Last night Bea came to dance and joined the party at our house. My Matt always catches huge salmon and trout in Lake Michigan and we have them smoked for our delicious buffets. Alex has become a winemaker, using Door County cherries that we glean from the trees after the harvest, pears from our huge tree in the back yard, and whatever else he can find. His buddies Bob McGregor and Pete make wine too, and we always have a generous supply for our parties.

As usual, the wine numbs some of our inhibitions in joyful celebration of whatever it is that each of us wants to salute, but it seemed that it hit Bea harder than the rest of us, perhaps because we ate food with our wine—and she didn't.

Always the one to spot a needy woman, Pete Kramer quietly made a pass at Bea that she thought about accepting at first, but refused. She'd been faithful to Jake for all these years: Jake, the quiet man living in a self-contained shell who needed only predictability to sustain him. Spontaneity and creativity scared him.

Most of the adults with younger kids left the party before midnight, but the teens and single adults stayed on to enjoy the company, the food, and the full moon shining on our house and on our Lake Michigan view. As is my custom when I can—especially on warmer nights, I walk my friends to their cars, give them a hug, and wish them well on their way. I walked Bea, the last to leave, to her car parked under the streetlight and warned her about making a U-turn because our dead-end road was also on a bluff with the lake below.

I gave her my usual hug, but she turned it into a long embrace.

She whispered in my ear, "I feel abnormal. I need to be accepted and to want someone to respond to me?" She wept when she told me about Pete's proposition, saying that she'd been looking for someone to add flavor to her life, and if not flavor, at least a break in her meager diet. "It is tantalizing," she said still holding me, "to find another person to fill my empty life, but it won't be that Pete."

I sensed Alex's eyes staring down from our bedroom window.

"It's tantalizing," she spoke in a lower tone, "to weigh the pros and cons of an affair and my battle with my husband."

I didn't know how to react, so I mumbled some dumb generalizations.

"I love you, Jan."

"That's what Alex doesn't understand about me. I love people."

"Oh Shit!" she said, finally releasing me. "I'm sorry. It's just another one of my frustrations."

Suddenly, she turned from me. Looking shaky yet confident, she folded her slim black silhouette into her driver's seat, turned on the ignition, the headlights, and spun a dusty U-turn to drive away.

Caught off guard by her intimacy—and her grip on me, I looked up to my bedroom windows to see if Alex was watching but I didn't see him. I came inside, put away the perishables, checked the fireplace damper, turned off the lights and climbed the stairs to our bed.

Betty Rock Willing

You are a star child, Capricorn, a star child
temporally born upon this earth to carry the
weight, to span the girth of all that needs to be held
and borne— Our Capricorn—so frail, so weak—
What a load to be twinned on Christmas eve and
lost in half like half a savior without promises of
immortality or even of a following.

Would you on another planet, another time,
to other parents, be the same
one who weeps and seeks a love in
 magnitude compared to yours?

"Star-crossed?" as the playwright says, and you
search
for a lover equal to your star-crossed fate.
Should you find one to parallel you, perchance
two star-crossed comets would fall beyond the scene
past old wounds, beyond our view and on to new
places having quiet lights and warm, soft spots
to stop and rest and comfortable places
with people so dear that you need to search no more.
From Jan to Betty (date unknown)

Jan on November 1, 1973

Betty Willing is getting to be a closer UU friend with her wild imagination and playfulness despite the chaos that seems to follow her wherever she goes—like a poltergeist.

Betty is divorced and always brings her baby daughter to church, tightly wrapped in a blanket, and she hands her over to the men to hold during the service and coffee hour. That way, she said, her baby gets to be held by men. Otherwise, she tucks the curly red-haired infant under a pew so she won't be stepped on.

Betty's a poet, a sculptor and a violinist with a great many ailments. Somehow she qualified for Social Security disability that supports her and her teenage daughter and now the baby. She's also a dear friend of our church organist, Em Kulper. They make a cute couple. She's about five-foot-seven, slim and blonde most of the time and Em is a blond-haired little person, sort of square in stature. He suffers physical pain but between the two, they laugh a lot as they drink and gossip together.

Betty unexpectedly appeared at our home one night to show me some of her poems. I was doing the laundry and invited her to come down to the basement. We could talk with more privacy there without Alex and the kids watching TV—and I'd get my family's laundry loads done at the same time.

A few days later, she invited me to come to her house along Lake Michigan in a wooded area on the southern edge of town "and we could talk some more," she proposed. She picked a full moon night, the same full moon that I celebrate in my lake view and I said yes. We took a walk among a few mature trees to the edge of the eroding, steep lake bluff and talked about feelings, poetry, and books that we've read while savoring a glass or two of wine.

"Betty, why don't you come to our adult education session, a Transactional Analysis Intensive, overnight this weekend at Emerson House? Bea, Marge, Anna, Roger and more are coming. You must have read it in our newsletter. There are still a few openings if you want to attend. I'm excited about it."

"I don't think I want my transactions to be analyzed but— Hum! Roger, huh? I'll think about it, Jan. That should be more interesting. I'll see if I can scrape up some money for the fees."

When Betty and I talked a bit about Marge, she implied that she didn't trust her and didn't want to get involved much with her. We talked about other friends and then about Bea.

"Once after coffee hour at church, I asked Bea if she'd written anything lately and she barked at me."

"I know you're only well-meaning when you ask me that, but your question makes me want to cry! First of all, I'm going through an emotionally trying time, full of personal problems I won't bore you with, except to say they're deep and, for me, critical. I keep telling people that I've been conditioned by rejection slips—and am not doing that anymore."

"What the hell! You don't need to jump on me. I have emotional problems too but I'm ready and available if you need encouragement, or support. You're like a sister, Bea. Come to our poetry group; they're mostly sensitive and helpful with their critiques."

But Bea declined. "These emotional problems prevent me from risking myself again with my writing. I'm suffering from an internal dialogue so painful that I think sometimes I'm about to fly apart. Part of me says, 'You can write, damn it. You're good!' The other part says, 'Oh yeah, then how come you keep getting rejected? It's because you're a lousy writer who has nothing to say, so for God's sake, don't kid yourself—or anybody else either.'"

"Well," said Betty, "I'm only trying to offer some help."

"The terrible part, Betty, is that no amount of outside praise or criticism can make a difference. It's in me where I get all twisted. I hope I'll express my words again. It's a compulsion and I must be strong enough to risk rejection."

"Shit! I'm no stranger to rejection. In addition to my stacks of rejection slips, even my own son walked out on me and went to live with his father!"

"Betty, I'm sorry. Forgive me for biting your head off because, as you can see, it's my own head I'm biting off. The second thing about your question is that it makes me feel guilty. Guilt argues with my fear of risk and tells me that I'm lazy and I'm wasting my talent. Get busy! Get to work! If at first, you don't succeed, shit!

Thanks for your help. You're a good friend. Please bear with me." Then she quickly walked out the church door.

Jan on November 13, 1973

Tomorrow's my 41st birthday, yet I'm being reborn during our TA workshop. How much courage does it take when it comes time to put your life on the line and say what you think?

When it was my turn to address my issues, I focused on my marriage. That was much safer than revealing my major anxiety, my secret love for another woman that could've been quite obvious to some when I jump up to inflate Marge's sleeping mattress, bring her snacks and fill her glass. I even treat her mother, Nina, with the same services.

Bea came dressed in a skin-tight body shirt and slacks with flared cuffs, all in black except for a silver metal belt around her waist. She whispered and asked me if I were Marge's slave. "I love doing things for others," I responded. "I'm conditioned to do that at home."

A simple technique that I should use at home is taking a pillow to yell at, twist and pound. And yell I did sitting cross-legged on the floor and twisting and pounding the pillow, thinking and pausing to express my emotions with the right words as each pounding kicks dust from the carpet. "I demand equality in my home." Smash! "I refuse to be put down" Bang! "To have my work, my important work merely tolerated!" Boom! And I caved onto the pillow.

Rachael urged me to go deeper. "Remember, Jan. Misery is optional."

"I'm not a slave to him, nor am I his subordinate. I want to be free of this negative drain on my energy. Continued self-sacrifice isn't the answer!" I shook the room with my fury. In time and with tears and exhaustion, I collapsed back against the sofa and found myself between Betty's knees as she leaned over and hugged me to give me comfort. As I regained my composure, I felt her legs growing tighter about me until I could barely breathe.

Randy King, who came because of our friendship and my enthusiasm over TA, passed when it was his turn to address his issues.

Rachael stayed at a hotel while we continued talking and many finally slept at Emerson House. Betty and Roger disappeared into the attic. Randy went home.

We regrouped on Saturday morning with an opening game where Marge gave me some written strokes on the cards we wore for all to see. We were to list our most precious gifts in the upper right.

Marge wrote on hers: "Myself, my children, participating in life, my friends." At the bottom right in a place of honor, she printed "Jan C." Her top left listed high points in life: "giving birth," "falling in love recently," "discovering that people like me." In the lower left, the "pit" part of the card, she printed "ex-husband."

Before the TA session, I slipped Marge a note. "I am and yet I only am when I am with you." She read it, smiled at me and put it in her pocket.

I treasured my "Strokes" that the fourteen others wrote. In grade school, my classmates circulated a "slam book" that gave others the opportunity to write ruthless messages on the page labeled with your name. "Strokes" gave me only good messages like: "You can." "Power abounds." "I wish I had such friends." "Hang in there, Baby." "Keep trying." "You're beautiful." "You're great as you are NOW." "I'm so damn jealous of you!!!" "Life is earnest; life is real."

Rachael wrote, "You have strength and you use it, but it's OK to be weak sometimes too. You give and you receive much love both ways." Betty wrote, "Keep trying. You'll make it." Marge wrote, "Stroke. Stroke. Stroke—M." Bea wrote, "I love you Jean, Bea." But most curious was a TA stroke in Randy's handwriting, "Please save a night for me."

Bea appeared even more frail when I saw her at church on Sunday. We all were. Before I went to sleep at home on Saturday night, I edited the little poem I had slipped to Marge, signed it and slipped it to Bea: "I am and yet I only am because I am with loving people like you. November 14, 1973."

Bea on November 15, 1973

I went to Lakeshore Bay for a Marathon Transactional Workshop with Rachael Sandler, the psychologist. Wow! To have someone reach down your throat and turn you inside out. To be stripped naked of your defenses. To give and to get. It will take me a while to recover. It was terrifying and it was marvelous.

I've always been wary of psychobabble trends in popular psychology, especially when the traditional psychologists who've analyzed my dad have been giving me the run-around about his mental conditions—his brains being scrambled and all that crap. But I'm so desperate that I gave this a try and now I feel opened up, yet still coming down, thinking, mulling its meaning.

I didn't want to open up in front of all those people, but Rachael drew me out. I'm a classic example of the women's dilemma. I've been a professional parent for almost twenty years. But I know I'm also an intelligent and proficient human being, but I've chosen to devote my life to raising kids the way they should be raised with my full concentration and total effort.

I felt the Lib movement crippled us women who chose parenthood, and motherhood, as a career. And in a way it does. Rachael rocked me several times off my original decision. She told me I should have a job. I know—for my own self-respect, I should have another identity. And that is most of the problem with my own mid-life crisis. The empty-nest syndrome. I must establish an identity.

I was looking for a job in the same profession I had originally chosen, mothering. I finished my degree in education, but I ended up without a job because of the abundance of teachers. I was lost. My mothering profession isn't honored anymore. I was going to find a job, knowing full well I would still have to handle the home, the cooking for six people every single day, doing the eight loads of wash once a week—the endless chores of cleaning and homemaking we're stuck with. And then there's my father and my husband to consider. I'm so damn involved.

I'll have to go out someday and become some other person. Meanwhile, my profession is an honorable one, that my identity and my life are still valid, and we who exclusively chose motherhood as a career are not to be pitied or helped, yet that is still a great need for us, as women, in the only real job that is totally natural for us.

In spite of our intelligence and our capability, our ancient job is still valid. I was a total mother. I was a den mother, a Girl Scout leader, a Sunday school teacher, and even a substitute teacher, but first of all, I mothered my kids to the best and most total effort I could put out, with every speck of intelligence and training I could offer them. I'll never know if I made better people out of them by doing that, by giving them everything I had to offer, but I had to do it. It was my career; it still is.

Can we be liberated mentally and be human beings in our own right while still being mothers? I had to get it off my chest. Another life is waiting for me someday, but I'm not quite ready yet.

At the end of the weekend, we were to write "stroke" messages for each person. Marge wrote, "Bea, I love ya." Rachael wrote, "Bea, I like you. Get what you need. You give much. Give to yourself too." Jan wrote, "Your potential is greater than your self-esteem." Another interesting one was "Very tempted to get your phone. Dig your body. Sincerely." Jan said later that it was Randy King's handwriting.

When we packed our belongings and started on our way out the door, Jan said goodbye, hugged me and kissed me smack on my lips. I was shocked. I knew Anna does that all the time, maybe because she's Italian, but I never expected that from Jan.

Jan on November 17, 1973

Today I sorted through the mail looking for birthday cards and I found a plain envelope without a return address and marked "Personal." Inside was a half sheet of white paper with a simple small message written with one word on each line, "On this warm November night, we could sit together by the lake in separate chairs and nobody would think it odd." A small hand-drawn mushroom decorated the bottom corner. A tiny tremor of excitement tingled through my body. What fun! Who could this be from?

My mind raced for hints of the many persons I had talked with and encouraged to express and share their deepest and most private feelings.

Could it be Marge—finally responding to me? She's creative enough.

Bea? She can draw!

My ego glowed. I've gotten non-verbal messages from others, but no one has yet risked this technique, this tempting written invitation. Its potential was exhilarating.

In the long-term security of my marriage to a loyal and trustworthy person, we had purposefully parented two admirable children without this euphoria—this suggestion of someone hinting at something beyond.

And I was interested. Society be damned—I was interested.

Jan on November 20, 1973

Bea called and asked to meet me for some Thanksgiving pie at 11 a.m. tomorrow at the Pancake House near Lakeshore Bay. I was happy to oblige. The first to arrive, I chose a cushy circular booth. She was trembling when she walked in wearing her lightweight navy—blue coat, a Coco Channel-style she claimed, with pointed collars lined in white. What do I know about styles? I ordered two coffees right away while we looked at the menu.

The aroma released an almost-burned toasty fragrance from its brown bubbles. The steam coiled in a smoky gray vapor around and over the earthen mug that warmed Bea's hands. She was still trembling, even more visible when she lit a cigarette. I ordered a pumpkin pie without the trimmings and Bea only wanted coffee.

"Maybe something hot to eat would warm you up."

"That won't stop my trembling and I'm okay. I'm fine. It's only the jitters, I guess, with all the stuff that's going on in my life. The TA stuff made me less tolerant of what I'm going through at home. And I'm open to new emotions as well. Here—" She handed me a small, gift-wrapped box. "I saw this and thought I'd give it to you."

"How thoughtful. But you didn't need to do that." I opened it and saw two children on an enamel pin, the black-haired boy standing behind a sweet girl with pigtails. They were holding hands. What made Bea think of me when she saw this pin? "Thanks for this. It's very sweet." Then I dared to say, "A small poem came in my mail," and gave it to Bea to read its one-word lines flowing down the page.

"On this warm November night, we could sit together by the lake in separate chairs and nobody would think it odd." I watched and waited. "It wasn't signed. Could that have come from you? Did you send me this?"

"No. I didn't write that. I usually go on and on when I write. Not like your little note that you slipped to me. I put that into one of my diaries."

The suspended pause lasted too long while I savored the warm sensations from her comment. I almost whispered, then swallowed and cleared my voice softly. I didn't know what to do.

Bea turned her head toward me, her eyebrows rising and her chin advancing as if in a dare, giving an expression that implied, "So. I told you something about me. Now let's play some more."

With a rumbling chuckle, I caught the mood, leaned back and laughed out loud. "My, but you made me feel good." I bent closer to Bea and gave her a gentle, sisterly kiss on the cheek. "Thanks for the pin." Her cheek felt so tender, so soft, the kiss so friendly and safe, yet intimate. Yes. Intimate.

"My, but you make me feel good," and Bea looked down into the steamy cup. Her cheek muscles pulled her mouth into a self-satisfied grin.

Bea was still trembling when we parted.

I spent many hours last night contemplating the immediate future: Can you relate closely to persons beyond the family without threatening members in that family? Can you afford to let a warm and intimate friendship slip away because you're afraid of what might result? Can you risk what you have? Can you risk losing what you may be missing?

The Transition toward Selfhood: A TA Resolution

- I must stop expecting from others as much as I would give of myself.
- I must stop expecting others to respond as intensely as I.
- I will ask for what I need rather than wait for others to guess what it is and then be disappointed when I don't get what I need.
- I can love and care for others but I must not feel responsible for them.

- I must ask what I can do for them and if I can't give them what they need, I should say so without feeling that I've failed them.
- I can only be responsible for myself and I'm cheating others out of the feeling of being able to be responsible for themselves.

CHAPTER EIGHT

Jan on October 5, 1973

My city editor asked several of the guys in the newsroom to take on this ground-breaking assignment but they were too busy, they said. When he asked me to do a breakthrough feature article on homosexuality, I said yes. He gave me no leads, so I started my research from scratch, reading some issues of a simple but straightforward Milwaukee's gay/lesbian newsletter I picked up months ago. I also drove up and down our town's seediest street looking for a place called "Jamie's Bar" that was so hidden I never found it. That was frustrating but somewhat exciting to think about entering this place on my own.

Alex didn't know about this assignment and my father told me not to do it.

A psychologist consented to be interviewed on the subject and suggested a client for me to interview. The gay man spoke to me openly and was generous with his time. Based on that, for starters, I continued my research and submitted half of the series. I said I'd get to women later, that is if I could find a lesbian.

My editor wanted me to finish the lesbian interview before printing the article—or series, but I couldn't find a lesbian. (Much later, I heard the rumor that his daughter was a lesbian but he never volunteered that information to me.)

My life continued to get even more hectic and when my city editor told me he needed to cut back on staff, I was happy to leave the newspaper and concentrate on St. Luke's and other projects. We always seem to be at some crossroads in our lives. As one road is crossed, another waits, each with its warnings or stop signs, flashing signals of yellow, green and red. He did ask me to complete the unwritten homosexual story I started and turn it in ASAP. But I never finished the article. I guess the subject became too personal for me.

The series was never completed; nothing was printed.

This is the first part of a draft I submitted to my city editor.

"Homosexuality in Lakeshore County"

Draft of Part One: I can also consult with Dr. Ferris on more Lakeshore angles, on VD and homosexuals, etc. I also want to talk with the DA on the criminal aspects and maybe a parole officer about prisoners in jail, and I also have more information from Dr. McHenry on how one becomes homosexual and what society should do. Another aspect to cover is the Gay Liberation people and how they celebrate their homosexuality. I can talk about the Milwaukee scene and try to find out more.

The article begins:

Homosexuals dream an impossible dream as they search for "the one unobtainable thing, a stable and loving relationship," described Dr. Walter T. McHenry, a Lakeshore clinical psychologist.

The average married person would be hard put to imagine the unhappy, lonely life that homosexuals live while looking for emotional and physical gratification in hit-and-run meetings, one-night stands, short-term relations, and a "triangle of men competing for each other's affection," he said.

"With a few exceptions, they never have the same chance as a heterosexual to develop a consistent relationship. It's a tragedy." With behavior rejected as loathsome by the American public, the gay world can be pretty glum and lonely. As a homosexual, he or she is considered with contempt not as a human being but as a fairy, faggot, fruit, queer, queen, dyke, or butch.

Yet a significant number of people are homosexuals.

Dr. McHenry said that the highest estimate would be that one out of seven men is homosexual. The lowest number would be eight to ten percent of the population. National totals indicate that eight to twenty million persons are homosexuals.

A Lakeshore County ratio is typical of that national figure, he said.

"Not all male homosexuals are limp-wrist Nancies. You can find them anywhere and everywhere." Male or female homosexuals do not necessarily dress according to stereotypes that would endanger their livelihood. Those who wear striking feminine and masculine attire are playing a role they think society wants them to play but their private lives and behavior could expose them to economic and social ridicule.

A Task Force on Homosexuality appointed by the National Institute of Mental Health reported in 1969, "Homosexual individuals can be found in all walks of life, at all socio-economic levels, among all cultural groups within American society, and in rural as well as urban areas. Contrary to the frequently held notion that all homosexuals are alike, they are in fact quite heterogeneous.

The reports said that efforts should be made to educate the general public because homosexuality remains such a taboo topic, an area where much misinformation abounds. "As such, it can create pervasive anxiety as well as condemnatory and punitive attitudes that could be prevented or eliminated if valid information about homosexuality was disseminated."

Dr. McHenry said, "Society labels as homosexual one who has had even one homosexual experience. However, a homosexual is one whose primary mode of sexual contact is with members of the same sex by preference. This can be either overt or fantasized."

The prefix "homo" comes from the Greek meaning "the same as," not from the Latin word for men.

McHenry explained that persons who prefer same-sex behavior vary in degree. "One is a person who lives openly as a homosexual and travels in the company of other homosexuals. The second is he who hides at home and moves and acts through secret meetings in bars, men's rooms, etc."

County areas for meetings of homosexuals includes two gay bars, one on Center Street and another on Master Drive, and two county parks on Highway 20. The men's room in Bryer Park is one other contact point. In Milwaukee, there are at least 14 gay bars and recreation areas and two churches and parks where homosexuals meet.

Dr. McHenry said, "Most men have homosexual feelings and fantasies, but they are afraid of these feelings and of enjoying them." This fear verges on panic, Dr. McHenry explained. "This panic over homosexual feelings keeps men from having a full, affectionate relationship with another man. Tenderness must not surface. That is too bad."

The lives of most American men are bounded by this constant necessity to prove to their fellows and themselves that they are not homosexual, and relationships are colored by this fear of their own potential homosexuality. He said that European men do not feel this way as much as Americans.

The person who prefers same-sex behavior in reality or in his erotic dreams differs only in dealing with others and the law. Purdue University's sex educator, Dr. James E. Moore, wrote, "We do not persecute people for what they think but for what they do. The law may be concerned with the intent of motive to determine relative culpability (blame), but in the final analysis, it resorts to dichotomy, guilty or not guilty, homosexual or heterosexual."

McHenry illustrated this fear by relating an incident that happened in this area. An adult man was picked up in a car by a woman who proceeded to give him sexual stimulus and gratification that the man enjoyed very much.

When he discovered that his sexual partner for the interlude was another male in drag (in woman's clothing), he definitely panicked, McHenry said, because he had enjoyed the act with a homosexual.

"It's a matter of what you think you're doing."

McHenry said, "Homosexuality is not a crime of violence and when a homosexual is 'cruising' for contacts and asks someone to respond to him, it sets off a complex set of emotional reactions. When a bum asks for a quarter, you can tell him to go away, to leave you alone, and you don't bother anymore with him.

"But homosexuals bring out violent reactions in many and get beaten up by law enforcement officers and others because of this genuine fear of latent homosexuality in themselves."

Since such behavior in women is treated by society with a greater degree of tolerance, said McHenry, "society allows greater latitude for women to show affection, to share a home and to live together. Men who do so are suspect. "This greater tolerance for women who love each other maybe because society may see the situation as only temporary and not authentic. Many think the condition will disappear when a woman meets an attractive, eligible man.

Does lesbian behavior indicate fear or contempt of heterosexual relationships with men, or does it indicate an attitude freely chosen and freely adopted? This latter opinion is offered by French existentialist author Simone de Beauvoir in her book, The Second Sex.

Dr. McHenry said, "Homosexuality is not so much a question of choice as one of a learned pattern of behavior. A homosexual is taught by life's circumstances and knows no other satisfactory way to behave. It is not bad behavior as much as learned behavior."

Dr. Charlotte Wolff offers a recent view of lesbianism in her book Love Between Women, based on extensive research in a field that has been neglected in the past. She rephrases "homosexuality" for lesbians because of the intense emotionality a lesbian feels. Dr. Wolff coined the term "homo-emotionality" because she said women are looking primarily for a love relationship rather than primarily for sexual gratification. A lesbian perceives love with a strong romantic outlook.

Dr. Wolff said they tend not to be as promiscuous as most male homosexuals and are searching for a perfect love partner, not a sex partner.

Dr. McHenry said that was true, but men are also looking for that loving relationship.

Jan on November 27, 1973

Our Unitarian Universalist Church lost our minister, who resigned to take a pulpit in St. Paul. He said they made him an offer he couldn't refuse. Most of us were sorry to see him leave. During the search for a new minister, several of us celebrated the opportunity of writing and performing our own adult Sunday services. I was one of those most eager and a bit self-righteous over the privilege of creating programs and "preaching" to the grown-ups after my ten years of celebrating with the kids. No one seemed to mind my adult programs because then they didn't have to do the work.

Thanksgiving, to me, is the most Unitarian Universalist holiday of all the Judeo-Christian holidays. Not only did we celebrate it in church on Sunday, but I tried a ritual at home to reinforce the meaning of the day, as the Hebrews do on the Sabbath and their other holidays at their family table.

Our liberal UU denomination adopted and adapted a UU Thanksgiving as most relevant because it stands for the freedom of people to believe as they wish. Unfortunately for the American soul, the Pilgrims were more interested in preserving their exclusive relationship with their own God when they landed here from Europe than they were in tolerating others' alternative quest for religious freedom. Fortunately, our country's forefathers and mothers had the insight to separate state and church politics.

Hanukkah celebrates freedom too. Except for the difference in time and in settings, these holidays are similar. Oppressors demanded obedience and the oppressed battled for their rights—and won. Centuries of Hebrews celebrating their festivals with their families in their homes using symbolic foods and rituals cemented their solidarity and their heritage.

So in the spirit of all holidays for religious freedoms, I organized Jenny, Matt, and Alex to clean the house together and set our fine china and crystal on clean linen cloths—all brought home from Alex and my three-year tour of duty in Germany in the mid-1950s. We prepared the house and basement for fun and games, organized the menu for relatives to bring appropriate side dishes, and bought and prepared the remaining menu, including a full beverage bar.

I remember growing up having many empty holiday meals while one parent or another was ill or away, and this holiday I invited someone who had no place to be. Lee Prime, the gay guy I interviewed weeks ago, was the one I invited and I was surprised when Lee said he would come.

Last Sunday, our liberal UUs followed me in an experimental program called "In Praise of Life." Rather than hearing a sermon, one of our two sopranos added her voice in wordless melody to complement taped impression of what the unborn child may hear and what the child in labor may feel—the sounds of the infant's world and the singer's muted voice questioning life and its promise, and finally, the music and sounds of experiencing birth itself. Hazel Sawyer rehearsed hard to pull all that together.

After her performance, plus readings and hymns, I presented my slide and audio presentation of my friend Luanne's delivery of her baby when Dr. Zander allowed her husband, Pete, to stay with her during the birth of their first child. It was a historic first to have a father in the delivery room. Luanne, an RN, was happy to have me capture her birthing experience and prepare an audio-visual slide show that I presented at my church service.

It began with the mother's heavy breathing and showed her draped and ready for the baby to be delivered. With the movie theme from "Brian's Song" playing on the tape in the background, the doctor's voice began, "Don't push. Right there. Don't push. Don't push. Hold it."

"I can see the head in the mirror," the mother gasped excitedly, forgetting the strain of hours of labor.

"Tremendous—tremendous. Hold it. No more push now. Just pant—no push." (With each gentle command, my slides advanced, showing the progression of birth from a discrete point of view behind the mother's head.)

And there it is—a nice—(as the baby emerges a bit at a time.)

"—little—(as the baby pushes forward after freeing her or his shoulders.)

"—baby—(as the doctor with skilled hands catches the newborn.) "

"—girl!"

"Girl?" crooned the mother. Her voice held such loving inflections that she turned that one word into a song. "

A nice, little girl," said the doctor tenderly.

And the slides closed in to show a bloody, gray newborn with toes and fingers stretching with the uncoiling of her body in the new atmosphere of freedom—stretching and reaching for something to hold—being propelled away from security and into life.

The father's almost inaudible voice was heard. "Beautiful—"

"Beautiful is right," repeated the mother as the baby's small cry turned into her first full-lung yell that echoed off the sterile tiled walls to proclaim the beginning of her own new life.

In a quiet moment during the physician's ministrations, Luanne asked, "Does she have ten fingers and ten toes?"

And mothers in the congregation felt the pull of their memories as the images projected them through their own childbearing experiences. The primal pull of the memory of birth is the common ground of all human experience, either as the creator or as the created. The parents' concern for their child with that most simple question is so basic, the loving concern of parents, "Does she have ten fingers and ten toes?" And the child was crying in the midst—the first shouts at life, the trauma of leaving this suspended environment, the splendid safety of the womb, the brutal shock of passing through the birth canal to be ejected into reality—the universal experience of every human being.

"Sure has," the physician answered.

"Does she look healthy?"

"She sure does look good and healthy. You did great, Luanne. Just great! Congratulations to you, Pete. She's a pretty little girl. She's pretty nice. What are you going to call this little one?"

"Amy," was their mutual response. "Can we see her?"

"Sure can," said the physician and he thrust the baby forward with both hands holding her before her proud parents. "Here she is. She's a cutie pie." And he gently placed the baby on her mother's chest.

"She's so little," cooed her mother. "She looks like a woman too."

The slides advanced to show the father, masked and close to his wife's head, holding her hand and stroking her cheek.

The physician asked, "Is it nice to have Peter here, Luanne?" The physician had done them a favor by breaking hospital and physician policy that prohibited husbands in the delivery rooms.

"Oh, yes."

"Nice to be here, Pete?"

"You bet!"

And as the clock ticked away at the first minutes of this new life beginning, Luanne looked back at Pete whose hand continued caressing her cheek.

"I love you," she said as the projector light dimmed.

Jan on November 30, 1973

When my mother's well enough—that means stable and quiet—she's allowed to spend the day with the family. For years, my father called the state mental hospital at Winnebago, and now I'm the one to call the county hospital. The clerk said Mildred had been upset but she seemed fine now and could come home for Thanksgiving.

I hung up the phone. Too often, I hoped that she wasn't well enough. It seemed selfish, but after thirty-five years of having her in and out of the hospital, with the last twenty-five years being mostly in, my sensitivity to her unpredictable behavior made me so edgy that I could barely tolerate the strain.

Our family gave her love and attention during her visits, but it was I who seemed most emotionally vulnerable when she behaved erratically. I wanted to protect my children from witnessing the same traumatic scenes I lived with for so many years. That's one reason why I seldom took my kids with me when I visited her in a hospital or an institution where she was confined. The county hospital was close to everyone who was family or who used to be her friend, yet I was the only one to sit in that dull yellow, barren dining room during visiting hours, trying to tell her stories that won't upset her or to make some sense about what she said. When she was visiting at home, I was never free of the tension and anticipation of being responsible for my mother's safety and behavior.

I dialed my dad to tell him she was all right and would he pick her up? OK, he said. He'll be over in two hours.

The last-minute Thanksgiving preparations began. We were busy in the kitchen when Lee Prime rang the doorbell as our first guest and I put him to work making relish trays. We soon realized Lee was as big an olive eater as the children and they all snitched some in the kitchen. I had my olives in my martinis.

When Grandma and Grandpa came, the visiting shifted to the living room where drinks and hors d'oeuvres were generously served. With the fireplace glowing, everyone was warming up, inside and out.

Alex's two older brothers, their wives, and children came with bountiful platters and bowls of food. His widowed sister, Var, and her daughter, Sona, were always late. We would tell Var to come at three o'clock when the socializing was to begin at four, and they would still be late. "That's Var's claim to fame—and her only resemblance to Marilyn Monroe," would be the family's often-repeated, so-called joke. For years, I would become annoyed at the indifference shown by her lateness. We thought not to invite them; maybe it would teach her to be on time, but then I would be concerned about their being alone. Besides, I needed her to talk with my mother. Aunt Var was great at talking about little details and my mother would miss her. She always asked for Var. "Why not," I thought, "when Var could carry on a conversation with a rock."

I appreciated Var and Sona's acceptance of my mother. Mildred didn't scare them; they didn't try to understand what she would say—and how loving, sincerely loving, they were to her.

Var and Sona finally came loaded again with dishes of food that often duplicated dishes from the planned menu, or their Armenian flavors competed with the dishes prepared by others and by us. We'd ask or tell them what to bring; it didn't make a difference. One year we tried to anticipate what Var would make and did not prepare those courses. That year she came bearing only a frozen pumpkin pie that needed to be baked at the final hour, and we missed several courses of our traditional multi-course meal.

We introduced Lee all around and offered another round of drinks. The children had small glasses of Alex's homemade cherry wine, and Grandma was granted a large glass of soda with a touch of brandy. With her delicate system, that would last her a while.

About four o'clock everyone was called to the dining room table, an inviting, warm place overlooking the darkening November skies and icy Lake Michigan waters. The adults mixed about for a comfortable fit of bulky and lean bodies, mostly bulky. The cousins sat at an extended table nearby. Grandpa would help Grandma with her food. Her dentures didn't fit and she hadn't worn them for decades, yet she seldom cut her food into chewable sizes.

I stood at the table looking over the group: my stable and generous spouse, my handsome 12-year-old son, and my beautiful 10year-old daughter—both loving and wholesome inside as well as out, my abundant in-laws, Dad and Mother in their sad relationship and our extra guest.

By virtue of my pastoral leanings and donned in the sacred cloth of my apron that I forgot to take off, the room grew quiet when I began the reading.

"For the goods of the harvest, we give thanks."

I looked at the group and prompted them to say together, "Thank you." All were good sports to go along with me and all responded, except for my mother and Lee, who were surprised by my little ritual.

"Let us be thankful for our dependence upon the good earth," I recited from my script taken from a UU handout. My voice modified into an oratorical mode as I raised one hand. "Let us be thankful for our world of nature and our responsibility to care for it."

Again they looked for my prompting and said, "Thank you." Even those who were Catholic or Armenian Orthodox went along with me, but I sensed their impatience, so I deleted passages from my gratitude ritual.

As I passed a tray of sliced fruit that they tasted to symbolize the rich gifts of nature, Grandma said, "Who but God can tell what came first, the hen or the egg, the man or his egg, the woman or her egg?"

"Have a grape, Mildred. That's easy to swallow," said my father.

"Who is there among you," she continued, "who would say the hen is more important than the egg, or the egg more important than the hen, or man his egg, or woman hers, or male or female, one less important one to another. Man became blinded with his own importance, but are women are as one with God and cannot escape what God has put upon her."

Lee was somewhat surprised, but looking around the room, he could see that this had happened before so he became intrigued by listening to this frail elder woman's ideas.

"But man has taken God's will in his hands and has bent woman to his will and covered his sins with the weakness of his mind over his body and falsely added to woman's burden the weight of his own being. For woman is of God as God is of a woman—and all things here on earth, and they who slew her and defiled her and loved her too, in the way of the world, and shall not abide with God in Heaven!"

"Oh, come now, Mother," Dad said firmly while patting the back of her hand.

"Mother. Mother. Mother." She turned to him. "I'm afraid for all the dead children. I worry about them."

I quickly started passing a half loaf of bread and pitchers of wine and grape juice to the children in two directions. Tolerant of my experiment, each person broke a piece from the loaf, poured the ceremonial beverage into little glasses, and drank while I read louder, raising my goblet, "For all gifts of living and of times past and present—"

"The laws of life have been written," my mother interrupted. "They have reached the far corners of the earth. And what has man availed himself? Power. Wealth. Fame and Hatred!" And she raised her glass to her mouth and tossed back her small portion of wine with flair.

Responding quickly to her gulping break, I continued, "—for all the effort and hope and love poured into our lives—"

"Thank you!"

Mother continued, "Or man pursue love, eternal life and true happiness with all that which God has given him. The pursuit of happiness is not the pursuit of women and the fleshpots of the earth. You have been given laws. You have learned them." She started shaking her finger at Grandpa, who gathered up her hand and gently put it back in her lap. But she continued, "Why have you failed to abide by them? Forget you not that God gave the keeping of generations into the hands of women who also hold the heart. Look ye into your hearts," she declared, "and tremble for what you see, knowing how grievously God has been offended."

"Mother. Please. Relax," I pleaded, wondering how the children would take all this.

"How can I relax when I've just returned from shock and watched your children come back from being dead? They were all dead!"

"All right now! Settle down!" said Grandpa sharply.

With a sigh that began from my former ten-year-old child's scared insides to my 40-plus-year-old adult's extended sorrow, I began again but was interrupted. "How can a woman guide the ways of her heart?" She looked at them, questioning. "For she is as the wind under my hand—and the Devil's. And it's man's power over her that delivers her to one or another. For woman is the heart of the world and man is the power. Together they are complete, one without the other is uncompleted, even as you, without the Holy Spirit, are nothing," she gestured to me.

"Please! Mother. Help me! Let me finish so we can eat!" And I concluded breathlessly, "We raise our voices in gratitude and praise."

I raised an eyebrow to the others. "Thank you!" And some of them crossed themselves.

I put down my reading, dropped my shoulders, smiled, and said, "Thank God! Amen."

"Amen!"

Alex and his sisters-in-law rushed to the kitchen to get the hot food out of the warm oven and passed the bountiful platters all around.

"Thanks, Mom, for the sermon," said my son, "but I'm hungry. Bring on the turkey and let's eat," and the others added, "Amen."

I collapsed in front of my empty dinner plate and poured myself another glass of wine.

Dad cut up bits for a special dish for my "sibling" Chico, his Chihuahua who could come in the dining and living rooms while our dog, Pepper, was trained to stay at the edge of the hall carpet.

Grandma settled down with each spoonful of dinner, was the first one done eating and she dozed off in her chair at the table. With no rush to hurry the meal after waiting so long for it, they savored every flavor. Before I had eaten my first bits of food, the others were passing around second helpings. After they finished, the teenagers helped carry the remains of the food back into the kitchen and went down to the basement to play games. The women stacked the dinnerware and wrapped the extra food into dishes and packages for each one to take home, then joined the men who had settled down in the living room with brandy snifters to complete the Thanksgiving feast. Each one nested in a soft spot, and Grandma snored a bit in the corner of the sofa next to her husband with Chico on his lap.

When Lee knew my mother wouldn't hear, he looked at me. "My mother's a hypocrite. I really appreciate not being with my family today, although I did see my son this morning."

"I didn't know you had a child."

"Oh yes. I was married when I was 24 and stayed married for four years. After that experience, I realized that being gay was the only way. I was divorced last year."

My father and Alex's sister were startled at what Lee had said. I'd not said a word about Lee's being a homosexual. I interpreted their thoughts, evaluated their reactions, and wondered, "Should I have introduced them to Lee by saying, 'Meet Lee—a homosexual.'" I smiled to myself thinking, "What would happen if I introduced my dad or Var to people saying, 'Meet my father and sister-in-law. They're heterosexuals!'"

Their post-turkey-dinner drowsiness disappeared with Lee's statement.

"He said it right out loud," Var must have been thinking, "not even trying to hide it from us." This might be the first homosexual person she has ever talked with, at least one that she knows for certain. "It's too bad," she said, "that you realized your condition after you were married, not before."

"Oh, I knew I was gay when I married. I've been a homosexual all my life, I guess, but my spouse didn't know. I don't even know now if my ex-wife is aware of my being gay."

"Well, why did you get married, if that's the case?" she responded, appalled at the irresponsibility of the deed.

"I married because I needed the security." Lee answered frankly without countering Var's hostile tone. "And I was ready to leave the gay scene behind me. I was tired of cruising and bed-hopping and competing for a lay, tired of the mechanics of being manipulated and of manipulating others. It's tough, truly tough on a person. Besides, I wanted desperately to have a child. Once I achieved that goal, I was happy."

Becoming more riled, she responded, "Manipulated! You manipulated your wife when you married her."

"Well, she's naive. Besides, I met with my priest and psychologist and they agreed it would be all right, providing I fulfilled my role in the marriage. My ex is getting remarried soon and seems happy. They'll make a good home for my son and probably will have other children of their own. I miss my son a lot, but I see him once a week. I missed him at first. I thought I'd die of grief, but I'm surviving. He's better off where he is now."

Speaking calmly but firmly, Lee emphasized, "If it weren't for my son, I'd really lay myself out for trouble and fight for gay people who are persecuted by society because of their orientation. Besides, playing both sides of the fence was not satisfying. When I decided that my lifestyle was better for me, I discovered myself and I realized that I am what I am and I like what I like without thinking of guilt and sin."

Var started to pale slightly when I imagined that she mentally visualized or tried to visualize what homosexuals do. She grew quiet and was lost in her thoughts as she mentally stripped Lee naked and fantasized about what he would do with another man in bed—or wherever. "Excuse me," she said as she went up to the bathroom to relieve herself.

"Actually," Lee said to me with the others eavesdropping, "it was my divorce that brought me to the gay lib scene. After my wife and I separated, I was alone, empty—without a family, without my son. I cried for weeks until I reevaluated my life and said that rather than sitting alone in my house, I would go back to the gay community again.

"But this time, I found a new attitude there. We're organized now and many have a better sense of self. When I initially left to get married, four men in our area's gay community I left had killed themselves in one year because of their loneliness, mental anxieties, and guilt. The suicide rate in the late 1950s and 60s was high, but that rate's declining now because of our liberation movement.

"Anyway," Lee shifted position, "now I found a chance to look for someone for a one-to-one situation. I have several good friends, but I haven't found the right person for me. I'm not giving up though. I'm looking desperately for a lover, for a marriage partner. Too many gay people are still oriented to being promiscuous. They're not happy with one person. It takes people like me—responsible and tired of the exhausting pace, bad encounters and risks. For many young men, love is in the pants; it comes down to that. It's crude. People, straight people, see only the sex. They should try to understand what we think first, our minds, and our visions. We'd all have a hell of a lot better chance of accepting each other."

"Well, what happened to your wife while you were married?" I asked.

"When I got married, I intended to be completely heterosexual, but I couldn't cope with those sex games either. Even with your marriage partner—especially with your marriage partner—you manipulate. When we'd have arguments or problems, the 'hot beef injection' remedy wouldn't solve a thing. We'd battle and become irrational and confused and inept and begin punishing each other again with more sex games.

"After my son was born, the tension grew worse. We didn't even talk to each other. She filed for divorce and said things about me at the trial that were false—things the lawyers had arranged for her to say—false statements in front of the court, and I was so ready to be done with it all, I didn't care who was to blame."

My father sat quietly, listening to each word. "It must be awfully lonely being gay."

"You'd be hard put to imagine the lonely life it can be looking for emotional and physical gratification in hit-and-run meetings, one-night stands, short-term relationships that end up in intensely angry and fierce quarrels or are cut off with abrupt, cold breaks at the end."

"I can understand that," the elder said, looking at his sleeping wife, who has been married to him for forty-five years and has lived with him on and off for about fifteen years of that time, counting the months of being home between round trips to mental institutions.

"Yes, I can imagine. It's a lonely world."

When Var came into the room again, Grandma woke up. She needed to go upstairs, too, and stiffly but abruptly rose without help, straightened her dress, and marched out of the room. I went to the hallway to watch for her return trip down the stairs and Alex left the room to freshen the drinks.

In a few minutes, Mother returned to the top of the stairs, stood at the baluster, and I heard her say, "I had a friend. His name was Richard. They called him dead." And she descended to the main floor. When Mother saw the kitchen filled with the after-dinner mess, she plunged into the china and crystal and began piling the fragile pieces in the sink. In minutes, with everyone rescuing the precious chinaware, the dishwasher was filled and the room was almost back to normal. The kitchen activity interrupted the intense conversation in the living room, and it was small talk, party games, and Green Bay Packers TV football.

My muscles were taut cables when I woke up the next day. Stretching full length and touching the cool spots left beyond the body-heated portions of the sheets, my body strained in the delightful agony of being released from a stone-still position. I must not have moved for hours. Cramps hit the calves of the tensed legs and I immediately straightened my feet at right angles to my body. That didn't work, so I lurched out of bed to stand up and release the knots tied within my leg muscles. When I felt my tightened shoulders straining toward my ears, I dropped those shoulders low to exaggerated extremes, stretching my chin muscles and back, and then I threw my arms up with flexing fingers reaching to the ceiling.

It was good to feel every muscle, even if they made their presence known with aching pain. Grabbing a robe to keep warm, I turned back to the bedside to shut off the ringing alarm and found a scrawled message on a table. I remembered now, waking in the night to write on my notepad next to my side of the bed.

> I had a friend.
> His name was Richard.
> They called him dead,"
> Grandma said on Thanksgiving.
> She's my mother, true,
> but also mother to Richard,
> who at eight and one-half years was killed
> by a drunken truck driver
> three months before I was born—
> a real nightmare from her past
> blending with everyday hauntings
> as a "burned-out schizophrenic."
> If it weren't for Grandma,
> I wouldn't be here,
> things being what they are,
> and I'm grateful for that.

The alarm had jarred me, but not so much as the note that brought to focus images from the past, stimulated by the events of the previous day. The whirling memory of my hero brother I'd never seen seemed double-exposed against the photo of a half-alive pregnant woman with the child I was to be. The woman's face was as drawn and blank as her black dress that covered the swelling inside her womb. The birth was to have been a happy experience, a sister or brother for Richard, a daughter or son for her new husband.

But Richard was dead, hit by a car as he stepped into the street. My mother saw and relived it all over and over. And she almost died—first of grief and then of childbirth. I came to life, not in the violent process of natural birth but taken quickly by Caesarean section that left the broken woman wounded again.

My father didn't have to take advantage of Mildred's friend's offer to take me if my mother died. Mother lived, and we were both taken home where I lay waiting to be held and fed. I assumed that we cried together, the child in the crib and the suffering mother who could not respond adequately to both our needs.

"Somewhere, I decided I was going to make it on my own," I muttered looking at myself in the mirror. "I wonder when that was?" I turned away to join Alex for breakfast.

My ten-year-old Jenny wrote a poem, too.

> When I write a haiku poem,
> I'll write something sad
> about Grandma being in her hospital.

CHAPTER NINE

Jan on December 3, 1973

Christmas hospitality started early this year, right after we prepared the house for another Thanksgiving and Christmas season. Like an Army officer, I maneuvered my family with a plan that organizes the four of us to prepare the house for company.

I cut out a card circle with each of our names in a quarter, a child's name alternating with an adult's. I attached the circle through the center onto a letter-sized card that listed four cleaning divisions and tasks on each corner: kitchen, bathroom, vacuuming the entire house and dusting the entire house. We'd never get in each other's way when we're cleaning. After each housecleaning, the circle would be rotated a quarter turn. The system hung on the refrigerator and it worked quite well, except that sometimes several months went by before we did the tasks again. I didn't complain if the house was dusty. I wasn't totally responsible for doing something about it.
During the week after Thanksgiving, we shifted into the next entertainment mode and decorated our artificial Christmas tree, the fireplace mantel and the windows. We hosted Alex's business associates and their wives on the last Friday night of November and our close couple's friends on Saturday night. The house only needed the dishwasher to refresh our dinnerware and crystal from the

cupboards, wipe swipes across surfaces and vacuum the carpet if needed it.

I quarter-mastered supplies in plastic bags of carrot and celery sticks on ice for dips, chunks of sausage and cheese squares and salad fixings, simmered a Nesco full of Hungarian goulash, chopped and stirred a cauldron of bulghur wheat pilaf and served our town's famous kringle for dessert. We extracted the large coffee pot from the upper pantry. We filled the liquor cabinet. The dinnerware and crystal were in and out of the dishwasher, ready for more entertaining and I became a chef and restaurateur for the week.

It's good I have a part-time job that I can arrange around my social and family full-time jobs.

On Sunday morning, the refrigerator and cupboards had plenty of leftovers so, during coffee hour at church, I invited Marge, Anna, Betty and Bea to an impromptu brunch. Alex and the kids would be watching the Packer game in the family room and I'd have my own party with my close UU women friends.

They helped me set the table and put out the cold foods while the remainder of the goulash was warming on the stove. The kids and Alex could graze for themselves from the remains in the kitchen. Plenty of his homemade cherry wine was served and there's always more in the "wine cellar." We toasted to good health as we gathered together around our dining room table and ate and talked and laughed until someone noticed that the December dark night was creeping into the windows.

I teased Marge, asking if she may have sent me an unsigned poem about a warm November night and Betty almost choked. After Marge said no, Betty cleared her throat to get the attention of the group, "That's my work, Jan. I'm the poet and you oughta know it."

"I should have known, Betty, but getting an unsigned poem in the mail surprised me so. It is a delightful gift. I didn't know you could draw. Thank you, dear."

"You are welcome, my dear. I'm a woman of many talents and I'm happy you liked it," said Betty, looking at me with her impish smile and one-and-only elfin expression.

Naïve me! I should have known. She was trying to start something with me. I never thought that Betty would welcome another woman's attention and I already had my emotional bank filling up and flowing over. Betty and I looked at each other, connecting through a sly smile as Betty and Bea raised their empty glasses toward me for more wine while the others decided on more coffee before they collected their coats and made their way home.

Bea was the last to put on her dark red and gray plaid winter coat but instead of putting it on and leaving, she folded it over her arm, sat down on the stairs in the hall leading to the front door and asked me to sit with her for a minute. The minute stretched into a longer time as she told me about her frustrations and fears. "You are such a wonderful listener." I heard Alex grumbling in the kitchen. She whispered in my ear, "And your eyes are so blue—a person could go swimming in them," and she started crying.

I put my arm around her back and shoulders. "Don't you want some coffee to help you clear your head before you drive home?"

"No thanks. I need this feeling to overcome my depression of going home to Jake and all those teenagers."

Before Alex reached his limit and would tell her to go, I said quietly, "I have an idea. You drive home carefully now and we'll meet tomorrow morning at ten to continue this conversation, only the two of us. I have the keys."

Bea on December 4, 1973

"Why is it, Jan, that you—that we—can be more open and honest with almost anyone except our spouses?"

"I guess it's the risk of revealing hurt, smothered anger, old wounds—and destroying the long-term investment in each other."

We were sitting on my old sofa that I donated to the living room.

"You're a good listener, Jan. You say 'Ah Huh' in all the right places."

"I learned not to pass judgment on others."

"People feel your empathy and come away relieved and a bit closer to wholeness after talking with you. And you often risked something personal of yourself, to get closer communication and that must make both of us feel better."

I'd come for some confiding, some unloading of fearful emotions that were distorting my life. My mother died last year. My father is driving me crazy. After my mother died, he moved into different apartments that were either too big or too small for him. He missed his tools, he said, so he bought a small house. Then he had another stroke and they had to put his little house on the market because he's in a nursing home again. "We still have to get rid of his stuff. He was drinking brandy from a water glass."

"And I have other occasions of events that are frightening to me too. First, at the TA workshop, when I was talking about my brother being a homosexual and I said, 'There but for the grace of God go I.' You asked, 'You're not a homosexual, are you?' And I said, 'I don't know, maybe I am.' And then I have a blank space—from there until I found myself pouring another glass of wine and talking to

Roger. I have no idea what was said or what I said after that."
"You spoke mostly of your teenagers and mentioned your fear of loving one of your daughter's girlfriends."

"God. I didn't! Did I?"

"I don't think everyone picked up on that. I did—because I'm in love with someone too—and I'm telling that only to you. Bea, I am deeply in love with another woman—Marge. She knows it. I told her. And there's never been any physical contact. I feel like I'm just one of those courtly lovers, a cavalier or a knight from King Arthur's court. Please don't tell anyone else. I know what it's like to discover that you love another woman. I can understand. And I appreciate having a friend like you to talk about how it feels, how it hurts, how it makes me happy."

"Yes, I can understand. "I've never had physical contact with my daughter's friend, but she certainly does turn me on. She turns everybody on. I'm scared silly, Jan" and I held up two fingers to make quote signs around drunk. "When we were 'drunk' yesterday at your house, I remember telling you that you were beautiful—that I needed your intelligence. I've several blank spaces in my memory—where we embraced and I cried—all these are frightening. My terrible depression on the way home from your house after that folk dancing night a couple of weeks ago was not due to Pete's pass at me—but my telling you that I loved you, Jan and you're saying, 'That's what Alex doesn't understand about me. I love people.'

"The depression after yesterday's brunch, Jan, was obviously caused by the same problem, and other blurred ideas have entered my head. I must clear up a misconception you might have because of something I said; that Jake's not the only guy I've been in bed with. True! But I forgot to add 'before I married him.' Otherwise, I've been faithful to him for twenty years. Not that I haven't thought of doing otherwise during the bleak periods—and I've had some *interesting offers lately*. And secondly, I wonder if there still might be some repressed anger in *our* relationship and I wonder if it may have to do both with us and our own mothers and how we related to them."

Jan thought a bit and said, "The loss of my mother—even if she is still alive, has a profound influence on me, on my relationships and on the choices I make in my life. And I think that neither you nor I have grieved our losses."

Our talk was so free and intensely personal as we sat close, comforting each other. I summed it up: "This is the most honest conversation I've ever had." And I leaned toward Jan who had her arm around my shoulder with smooth and subtle body pressure. My head and shoulders eased softly onto the soft pillow on the arm of the sofa. Jan followed, breathing close, blending smoothly into one.

I remember Jan tensing to regain her composure and said, "I can't. I just can't. I can't be responsible for another person's feelings. I'm sorry, Bea, but I'm already so confused about what's going on. I can't let myself give in."

I too was relieved at the change in the intensity of our emotions. "Okay. That's good. Okay. I have to leave to pick up my kids from school anyway. I don't want to start anything that I can't handle either. Your emotional support is enough. As for Jake's support, it would have been better if I had been a number cruncher or a bus driver. Creativity is a threat."

"What drew you together then?" Jan asked.

"I wanted to have children. How about you and Alex?"

"I subconsciously chose not to be a lesbian after having a year-long affair with a more mature girl when I was in high school. I didn't truly know what a lesbian was. It was frightening but fun, especially in those days and it's still scary because of what people and society can do to you. I also wanted to lead a sane and normal life with a husband and children and I wanted the security that I never had."

Before we gave each other a cautious, caring embrace, I mumbled while I looked for my car keys, "...leaving me glowing but in emotional turmoil."

Jan on December 4, 1973

While driving home, I mulled over my marriage and its beginnings. *"When you're young, you look for love everlasting, but then you find reality, duty and responsibility forever."* And Marge and our one-sided relationship surfaced. *"Could loving Marge have released the fear and unlocked the potential for loving Bea? What about Marge? I still care for her. I think I still love her."* I was so absorbed that I barely missed hitting a pedestrian and almost sailed through a stop sign that I'd obeyed for years. *"I'm not prepared for the hassle with Alex and the kids. After flying so high, I must get ready to be emotionally shot down in the safety of my own home."*

Realizing the sensation of flying high reminded me that I was in the midst of reading Erica Jong's best-selling *Fear of Flying*, that wild, funny and passionate escapade of a woman wanting robust physical sex, emotional love and intellectual independence. I'd soaked up these revolutionary and uninhibited cathartic words while reading the book and it didn't take long to absorb Jong's fantasies created with the bawdy, liberated language used exclusively by male writers like Henry Miller. Jong's tales and other readings made it easier for me to imagine the possibility of having children and a career, domestic love with a man as well as unrequited and/or lusty love with women. Like a dreamy cavalier, I could get lost in thought about joining other worldly-wise women who celebrate having it all and making it work for themselves and for everyone concerned.

When Alex is angry with his bickering kids, he's always quiet during the exchanges, preferring to use an intense technique rather than shouting, but his anger would be revealed when his cheeks grew taut as his molars clenched together like a vise.

This time he was also angry with me: "Where have you been? Supper's not even started."

Though I tried to stay calm and neutral by getting lost in thought, those thoughts couldn't cover the rising pitch of our children's voices. I mixed a martini and went into the other room to read the paper. Everyone else seemed to follow me except for our dog Pepper, who crept into her crate.

They were arguing, of all things, about where to eat. It was a great idea at the start when Alex suggested it, but the entire scene turned into frustration when he asked the kids where they wanted to go. Hamburgers versus tacos; fish and chips versus family night at the steak house. No matter what would be chosen, someone would be unhappy about what was to have been a treat.

Before my drink was half-finished, I shouted, "For Christ's sake! Why can't people be kind to each other!" It rang like an alarm and startled Alex and the kids so much that they jumped. Surprised too, I laughed inside at their reaction: "I scared the shit out of them." And I didn't reveal even a ripple of chuckling body movement. I stood up, picked up my empty martini glass and returned to the kitchen. Now the dog was hiding under the table. "Did I scare you too? I'm sorry," and I reached into the cupboard for a dog treat and reached into the liquor cabinet for another treat of my own. "I love you Pepper," who received my peace-offering scratch with wagging forgiveness and appreciation.

Alex chose the all-you-can-eat buffet and when they had finished eating and walked out the door to the car, I, with hands in my coat pockets, tripped on a stone and fell between two parked cars.

I'd saved a cartoon in a daily newspaper series on relationships, clipped it and put it on Alex's dresser. The innocently naked little man stands by a grinning naked woman with her arms up in the air, showing elation and a broad, open-mouthed grin on her face; the printed copy reads, "Love is letting her be herself without your criticism."

And I mailed Bea this little note: "I can give you no cure when you tell me how you hurt. All I can do is care."

Bea on December 7, 1973

Life is sweet. I'm on top of the world. Joy to the world! Two most important days—Monday, with Jan and Tuesday, with Jake! First Jan for gentle romance, then Jake for sex. There was a storm on the lake, turbulent like me. Jake took me to the Yacht Club Christmas party. We drank. I was about to burst from sexual tension. I could not stand being deprived anymore. Jake and I blew the lid. Honestly and beautifully. Sex at last and the glow continued when we loved again.

On Wednesday, Josh and Joel took our donated furniture to Emerson House where we met Jan and Marge. We were all in a gay mood and had an impromptu party. More Love & Joy. Sunday church left me with a warm glow. When I got back home, more Joy! Kids. Joy! All of us were gay, laughing and joyous all day.

Monday was joyous again because Jan drove to meet me at my dad's house that we're selling. It didn't take her long after I called her to drive to see me and soon she stood near me, leaning against the wall and talking to me while I sat at the little folding table where I was addressing Christmas cards designed with Joy! Joy! Joy! on the front of the card. The house was almost empty. I'm selling it because my father was in the nursing home and they told me he would never leave.

She had poems and my letter I sent her yesterday and I had her notes secreted away in my little diary. I said something stupid like, "I don't know how women could be in love and how it works."

We were really high on our feelings for one another. I could see how nervous she was, smiling at me. From her standing near me, I sensed her tenuous joy as she looked down toward me and my Joy Christmas cards. We each were aware that something was going on. Maybe this was something we could allow to happen. We were both still married with children. We talked in terms that we used from Eric Berne's *Games People Play* and from our first TA session and we talked about our writing to each other.

I forgot to offer her to sit down, but we'd sold almost everything in my father's little house. I stood to show her the place. When she told me it was time for her to leave, I touched her hand and, as is customary with so many of us women friends, I only wanted to give her a hug. She must have felt me tremble against her and she quickly stepped away.

"I don't know what to do," she said as she touched her lips on my cheek and said goodbye like any family friend would do. If I had been prepared and quicker, I could have turned my head only fast enough to catch her lips on mine, but she had already smiled and backed away.

That was it.

Bea on December 12, 1973

Dear Jan,

You didn't reject me! You rejected a lifestyle you've been thinking you would like better than what you have and would make you happier than you are now. Maybe you don't even know it yet. Like you probably don't realize how you encouraged me to take us to this point. We're both responsible, but I do have to take my share of the blame because you're right, I was playing TA's "Wooden Leg" game. How can we ever stop playing games? You were playing "I'm only trying to help you." I know you wanted me. You said a lot, all over the place and since we both, as women—Women, Normal, NORMAL WOMEN—hunger for the same things, especially at our time of life and mind and because we live life with more gusto than some, it has to happen. But it didn't happen, either. Think about that. Ask yourself that same question you claim to have answered to your satisfaction. Do you truly want what you think you want? I ask myself all the time, "How can a person as intelligent as I am be so damn stupid?" You do love, Alex. You always have. Let's not talk about futures; but because we don't actually understand love, we think it's something else than it is. You accuse me of projecting my thoughts from yours. I was, you were and you are. Let's stop being "Disguised as a Normal Person" and admit to ourselves what we have.

I know I love you, but not sexually. And yet I do because sex has nothing to do with love—and everything.

For your secret life—

I'm walking around in a blue fog with a million other things to say to you. Dancing on housetops. Flying over fields. Singing from the bottom of the sea. You are the mother who rejected me when I needed her most, the sister I never had, the friend I needed most, the love I thought I wanted.

I thought Tuesday would solve something. Then I came home and found your card. So I wrote one back. I discover often that I'm a great mimic and imitation is the greatest form of flattery.

You're OK, Jan. Be honest with yourself, too. If I'm OK suddenly and I am the reflection of you, you're OK. You make me want to mother the shaky little child that's hiding and peeking out from under the facade of strength and power.

>Joy, love endless.
>Bea
>Ask yourself what you want and give yourself an answer.

Jan on December 26, 1973

In my joy of the unfolding of a happier aspect of myself, I sent Bea this poem and then read it aloud as a Sunday morning Christmas worship service that I organized while boldly striding across the church sanctuary, almost as if this space were my courtly castle chamber and I was adorned in regal robes and a wide-brimmed feathered hat.

"Celebration"

"I think one must finally take one's life in one's arms."
After the Fall by Arthur Miller

"… and reach out to the risk of living with both arms. One has to embrace the world like a lover."
The Shoes of the Fisherman by Morris West

> I have taken my life in my arms—
> I embrace the world and sense its pulse as
> I feel in oneness with the beat of life.
>
> My legs stretch to keep the pace, my heels
> vibrate with each determined step as I dance
> each moment to the meaning of life.
>
> My self reaches out to be itself I risk loving
> those who accept that self as I live, as I
> consume the full measure of life.

Alex looked as if he were thinking, "What the hell does that all mean?"

<<<>>>

I'd taken over the Christmas Eve church pageant from another woman because I thought my ideas were better than hers. Marge and I schemed this program during a folk dancing party when I suggested we use Don Bolognese's *A New Day* with a Mexican Christmas story rather than the traditional setting. I chose Marge to be pregnant Maria and our fuzzy-faced friend Pete Kramer to be Jose. Instead of shepherds and wise men, we had a motel owner, a gas attendant, three cowboys, folk dancers and singers, including Matt and Jenny, David and Timothy, the Dixon kids, the Spences and Kramer families.

Hiding in the church vestry, Marge as Maria needed to place a volleyball under her long dress and Pete was more than accommodating in helping her. While I was narrating the story, we could hear chortling from the mother-to-be and old Jose. The giggling settled down for "Silent Night" along with "It Came Upon a Midnight Clear" with the whole world singing back to the angels their song, "Peace on Earth, Goodwill to All."

From my place at the sanctuary pulpit, I scanned across the families of my church community with Marge in the Christmas play, Alex sitting near the back where he could serve as an usher and Bea, in a ruffled white blouse, long red skirt and leather boots, of course. Her daughter, Jill, was with her and they ushered themselves to the edge of the room. I'd heard her voice in harmony with a phrase in one carol.

The Kramers again circulated an open invitation to join them at their annual Christmas Eve open house in their little home that became jammed with this extraordinary mix of faithful, joyful and triumphant celebrators as we all wassailed together, young and old and my real and extended family of friends.

Happy Hanukkah, Merry Christmas and Happy New Year.

CHAPTER TEN

Jan on December 28, 1973

Yesterday morning Bea called me to say she had some tools to deliver to Emerson House and I could meet her there. "Yes, of course," I responded with a touch of wonder, and I left home speculating on what this was all about. I watched from inside Emerson House as her green Plymouth drove up the driveway. Bea jumped out of the car with a hammer and a couple of screwdrivers. "Ha! She wanted to drop off some tools and I thought she needed help carrying them in," I thought and smiled, knowing it was a lame but exciting excuse to meet me.

"You looked so fragile, Jan. I wondered how you've been?"
"I guess I'll be fine. I fell asleep on the sofa. Alex woke me at ten and I went up to bed and slept all night."
"Sleep could mean boredom as well as exhaustion."
"Yes. A lot of anxiety about Marge and about you—and me too."
We talked for over an hour about our lives and feelings. I stood to go to the bathroom—and to think. When I returned, Bea rose and stood close, directly in front of me. "I couldn't sleep all night. I kept thinking that I only wanted to hold you like a small child that you are and give you the comfort that you need." We embraced each other gently.

"It's so different holding someone new," I thought. "Each body contour fits in new places against mine." And while I was analyzing these new sensations, I felt a shudder escape from within Bea, who pulled back immediately and turned away. "What's the matter?" I whispered. "That felt so fine, so kind, so close."

"I'm only here to comfort you. That's all I want to do."

"Yes. I know. And I appreciate that."

In this tender and protective manner, we stood holding each other for a long while.

Magnetic tension made it inevitable that we would become more deeply involved despite the fears of what could happen if we did. Whatever it was that drew each of us together during those weeks before this day, it was as if the energies of a lifetime that were held inside of each of us could not be contained—a power surging to envelop us.

I asked softly in her ear, "What could it hurt if we just let it happen?"

As if electrified, she jerked back to be eye-to-eye. "Jan! Oh no! We can't do this! It could hurt you and it could hurt me and everything we've lived for. In spite of your proclamations of strength, you're not strong enough for this—and neither am I!"

In fearful rationality, we tried to think—to hold back. I believed, *"What could it hurt if we just let it happen."* I remained in a daze, in a blur, so bewildered that I couldn't clearly remember. I focused only on holding her as we stood in the middle of the room and then, finally, finding her mouth, kissing her soft, willing lips, kissing me in return.

We found each other. A lifelong need too long repressed electrified both of us. There is no going back now.

Bea on December 28, 1973

Dear Jan,

I have something for you, something that may save your life, that may save your marriage if you can listen and, Dear God, if I can only give it to you right. I have to start at the beginning, I guess, but where is there ever a beginning at this time of life? I got drunk last night, blessedly drunk! And slept beautifully. Woke up at 4 a.m., had two more drinks and slept. But somewhere in there, I wrote something. So tonight, I'm reading Herman Hesse's *Siddhartha* that you gave me—for what reason now, I don't know? And out drops this paper that I don't recognize. I never saw it before, I think. I must quote it because I'll keep it and treasure it. It says, "Hit the road, Jake. I'm me and you're you. I've never owned you and you've never owned me. I love you but you will never, never own me—ever."

I came across Ayn Rand's *The Virtue of Selfishness* and here is a quote you must read. "Love and friendship are profoundly personal, selfish values. Love is an expression and assertion of self-esteem, a (I can't see because I'm crying) response to one's own values in the person of another. One gains a profoundly personal, selfish joy from the mere existence of the person one loves. It is one's own personal, selfish happiness that one seeks, earns and derives from love."

Therefore, Jan, requited LOVE must really be impossible— and perhaps meaningless. It is there, but you or I or even anyone can never acknowledge it because it might destroy it. Does that make any sense?

You encouraged me. I wouldn't have dared do what I did otherwise. Think about it. Listen to what was said and what clues I heard and fell for. But I'll never regret it. I learned something you need to learn. It may free you even more. You don't want what you think you want. "Give to yourself," Rachael said that to me. She wrote, "You give much—Give to yourself, too!"

Jan—don't throw your life away without consideration. He's always loved you. How could he have married you otherwise?

You cannot be comforted for the same reason, but if you need it, if you ever want it, I'll be here. I'll always love you and want you on different levels—because you are me and you are not—you are life and you are death. You are safe and you are danger. The Yin and the Yang. The Alpha and the Omega. The Beginning and the End. I'm falling into the trap of mushiness and lack of clarity. Isn't it funny?

Even my handwriting is like yours, or yours is like mine, whatever.

For God's sake, destroy this letter after you read it.

I'm going to mail this now, immediately before I have time to reread it or rethink it. I need it. I think you do.

There will always be love between us.

Jan on December 28, 1973

Dear Rachel,

Do you counsel people privately? I'll be calling you to make an appointment so that I can get some details off my mind before we get into the workshop here on Feb. 1 and 2. I think it's important for you to understand the complicated emotional relationships among several people who'll be attending.

Some people have come to me for help and lacking professional techniques and a weakness for rescuing, I've gotten myself into a dependency problem or two that may explode at the workshop.

During our next weekend workshop here, could we work more on how to deal with a passive person? I gave my husband, among others, the longer version of the enclosed poem (Celebration) as a Christmas gift. It captures how I feel about myself and life and I'm happy and grateful to feel this way.

However, his response was that my present attitude (of embracing the world in my arms) is a liability in our relationship and that I must make an adjustment: that is, back to former feelings of resignation, resentment and boredom. During the course of our calm and one-sided communications, I asked him three questions that he did not answer but stared silently into space.

1. Do you love me for what I am or for what you want me to be?

2. Are you sure your reasons for being unhappy about my happiness are correctly labeled? (He cites duties as wife and mother, but I think it's envy at my wonderful response from my professional world and my human relationships with others. Also, he needs me to be exclusively his.)

3. What do you specifically want me to do? (Blank silence, staring into space, no word spoken for what seemed like twenty minutes.)

Finally, he spoke to a new point in the issue. He knows I know that he wants me to give up everything I am right now to be what he thinks and wants me to be and he can't say it because it's absurd. I won't change back and, by his own statement, I'm risking my marriage.

I'm going on too long now, but with all of us here knowing each other so well and going to the same church, it's ok to risk myself during our TA marathon, but I must not risk Alex who's extremely uptight about these TA marathons.

Jan

Jan on January 14, 1973

Marge and Bea are becoming close friends, especially when the demands on my time are so intense.

Our church is still between ministers so Alex is gone many Sundays looking for a new minister. When he isn't away listening to a potential minister preach as a guest in a church pulpit in another city, Alex and Matt go ice fishing. Or he's on another extended business trip.

The written and phone communications Bea and I share are crucial exchanges. In her writing, Bea waxes eloquently and uses language so scholarly I can visualize footnotes. Writing letters and poems fills those free hours if we cannot talk together. We exchange poems almost daily, and have clandestine meetings at our homes, church, Emerson House, wherever we can when we're not tending to our kids, husbands, friends and responsibilities.

Her frail emotions, endless frustrations and outbreaks of anger frighten me even though I know I love her. I also love Marge and her shrewd determination, sharp wit and concern for each of us, although she isn't fully aware of what's going on between the two of us. We both love Marge, each in our own way.

Suddenly, I was taken away from all this on a business trip with Alex to San Francisco that was like the honeymoon we never had. Of course, three years in Europe twenty years ago was a long honeymoon, but this week of enjoying San Francisco together reminded me of those loving years when we were more fun and free, equal husband and wife. It was good.

I met my now hippie artist friend Maria Grassie for lunch. I took the risk to tell her that my life was evolving and I'm becoming involved with women. My risking that information with her was a safe way to release some tension in me and rehearse that statement for the future. To my surprise, I may have actually shocked her.

I took my St. Vincent Millay poems and biography with me to enrich my time while Alex was at work. I found her poetry and her life story relevant to my life. That amazed and startled me. It gave me valuable insight to question my long-term unhappiness in my marriage and a short-term but intense attachment to women.

"Edna (St. Vincent Millay) found people and even lovers interesting mainly as subjects for her poetry. Her emotions about them mattered more than the people themselves, not because she was cold, heartless, manipulating, but because that was where the deepest drama lay—transmuted into poetry," wrote her biographer Joan Dash in *A Life of One's Own*.

"Her poetry was the siren call of a lonely woman longing for love and admiration and intimacy, yet once she had it, it was as if she had thrust her hand into a jar of leeches—they could suck her blood and drain her dry."

Though the quotes may be over-stated and dramatic, they reveal how excited, confused and afraid I am about my emotional state, my feelings for many people and my life. It shows how I may be projecting my fears of losing my children and what life is like being a lesbian, my mother's influence, instability and my dramatic interpretations.

In this creative rush that we're in, all the poems and songs are messages and the sharing is profoundly motivating when those you trust pay attention.

Bea on January 14, 1974

I talked with Jan and Marge at church today and Jan announced that she's going to San Francisco with Alex. That may give me time to recover from all the stress swirling inside and about me. I'm especially exhausted from Friday night's folk dance party. After only five glasses of wine, I was smashed as usual. Marge took me to her house. I got sick. I cried and drank coffee and talked to sober up—until 5:30 a.m. I got home after Marge drove me to my car, had three hours of sleep and rested all day Saturday.

I'm going to pieces, but I've gained some insights from Helen Reddy's *Long Hard Climb* that I gave to Jan earlier in the week. Now Jan is pissed because I hugged her for about ten minutes at the folk dance party and Alex was standing right there—watching. That's when Marge rescued Jan from me and then rescued me by taking me to her house.

My dad was released from the hospital. I took him to see the psychiatrist who told me his brains were scrambled and he would never get out. He would release my dad now but he gives my dad a fifty-fifty chance of making it. I found him a furnished apartment in his girlfriend's complex. What will I do with him? As usual, the kids are driving me crazy. Also, my doctor told me that I may have to have surgery and lose my guts; then a week later, he told me I could keep them.

Bea on January 15 and 16, 1974

Anger! Perhaps you had better examine your own ulterior movies the next time you want to play "I'm only trying to help you" and end up saying "What could it hurt if we just let it happen."

Who took who to Emerson House in the first place? Who ached to hold me? "Can I hold you? I want to hold you!" I wasn't feeling until then. After that, I can't stop feeling it! I can't shut it off! I'm caught in a paradox where intellect cannot rescue me. You want to absolve yourself of any responsibility for me! Okay. I know I would only have to be my own obnoxious self and I'd make you hate me sooner or later. It's healthier for you.

What about me? You took me where my defenses were down. I kept my coat on. It didn't help. I hurt, hurt bad and you wanted to help but in a way, you sensed I was defenseless. Blame me for that too.

I woke up Saturday after three hours of sleep with the most tremendous case of chills. I didn't go see my father at all that day. I wasn't in good shape. Rebellion? He scolded me for it the next day, or for not phoning him at least.

I'm filled with anger, for you especially. I kept trying to figure out why. "I didn't mean to love you." That's part of it. Then you were trying to involve me in your lifestyles where I didn't fit. Or let's say I had too many corners to knock off before I'd fit my square pegs into your round holes. And those corners were extremely painful to knock off, even if I felt I wanted to.

Besides that, you announced you were leaving me—for San Francisco and you were absolving yourself of responsibility for me.

Deal. Okay. (Damn! Damn! Don't repress everything please—Please!) I'll try not to. My mother left me a lot. She left me over and over.

Obviously, I must give you a chance to respond to this tirade.

I must have come along when your defenses were down too.

I did try to talk you out of it twice!!

"What could it hurt if we just let it happen."

I said, "It could hurt you and it could hurt me. In spite of your proclamations of strength, you're not strong enough for this and neither am I!"

Or don't you remember my saying that either? Then you came back from the john and said, "Yes, I guess if we let it happen, we both would be filled with such self-hatred we couldn't live with ourselves."

And I said, "Isn't that what I said?"

Or have you repressed the whole scene? Or is it me? God help us!!

Jan, I didn't want to love you. I told you, "I didn't want this—this love." I told you in our second session at my father's house that I felt responsible for the whole thing and had misled you by not clarifying experiences, but for God's sake, don't leave me standing here in adulthood all alone! You grow up too. Romanticism—

"Life is not a long song," sings Helen Reddy. I want—I want it to be!! I feel intensely!!

You sublimate me and turn me into putty. I can't do that anymore. My defenses are gone and I play no more games. I play no tennis. I play no folk dancing. I play no special games. I play for real. This is a relationship or it's not! You have the ball now. It is your serve. (I want to play tennis with you. I think it would be interesting. Even if you do beat me.)

I may have courted you subconsciously. I must admit I did play "Cavalier" with you, with hugs and compliments and empathy and sympathy. I had a qualified love, a friendship love. Then I was protected—until you held me—and the dam broke. A lifetime of emotion burst through me and no amount of hurried repairs or sandbagging can seem to stop the inevitable flow of feelings. I have too much time for it, and not that I can get back almost totally every time I replay the scene. Skyrockets! I said. Inside my whole body. Every neural synapse, every neuron fires—Shebam! And the violence of the passion returns again and again.

Then the kiss, the utter tenderness of that kiss, made eons of waiting worthwhile. The ache in my body does not subside, the desire to repeat the tenderness does not subside. Rationalization. Intellectualizing. Reasoning doesn't rescue me! Understanding does not keep my Parent from beating my Child to death about the whole thing either and I am torn nearly asunder.

I have not sobbed so hard—or been in such agony of—what, self-pity? I don't know—

"All you losers. You are a full-time blueser. If you're somebody that's feeling sorry for herself, better sing along." This is gonna be the last blues song in all my adult life.

Nothing has ripped me up as this has.

"A woman in love is out of her mind," writes Simone de Beauvoir.

A woman in love with another woman has got to be out of her fuckin' mind! It is suicidal. A passion like death. A primal desire to get back to the womb.

Still Wednesday

I only reread this for the umpteenth time and dated it and realized something odd about the date. Today was my brother's birthday. I haven't thought about that in years!

I feel like a dog chasing his tail! I go round and round and I'm getting dizzy. A whirling dervish! The agony and the ecstasy. Must they go together?

Existentialism. The philosophy emphasized the need for personal decisions in a world without purpose—a world in which loving someone can lead to dishonor—and killing someone wins medals.

"What a world. What a world," said Margaret Hamilton as the wicked witch of *The Wizard of Oz*. "That such a little girl as you could destroy such a powerful witch as I—I'm melting!"

I'm melting, too. Rachael Sandler told me once, "You're getting a lot of witch messages." That statement threw me for a minute. I was dressed totally in black, as usual. I sometimes think of myself as looking like a witch. The song "Witchy Woman" interests me. My children's novel had good witches and bad witches in it with the "power" of psychokinesis—and which witch is which?"

> "You've cooked an evil mixture.
> You've mixed a vile brew.
> You made your own juice, baby,
> And in it, you can stew."

At my first sub-teaching job last year at Lincoln Elementary, Southport's inner core school, a black kid came up to me and asked, "Are you a witch?" I said, "Sure! Of course I am," and he pretended to be scared and we laughed.

I go round and round and I never get anywhere. I keep having these recurring themes—trapped inside this lonely masquerade of life. Blank walls surround me on all four sides. I have no privacy. At home here, we suffer from overcrowding and poor scheduling. I have no place and no time to be alone—and I need it.

I want it and I don't—both!

Ever hear the "don'ts" that Helen Reddy has slipped in "Ruby Red Dress" while she is singing "leave me alone"?

"Yes. I know how lonely life can be."

Fourteen pages—See how easy it is for me to write novels. I only wish they would be any good, which they obviously are not. I wrote two completely. I have three others half-finished. I only reread one hundred pages of one yesterday called Red, White and Black and discovered what I had forgotten. Ten years ago, I had the same themes and the same feeling and the same conclusion. I'm not growing; I'm only growing tired and older.

"Tired of livin' and feared of dyin', Old Man River—" Old Lake Michigan. He just keeps rolling along. I have to go and look at "him," my beloved lake. Water of Life. Water of Death.

Why oh why did my brother have to choose that way to die!!! Because my mother said, "You go jump in the lake," and he did.

I shut it off with alcohol. It doesn't work. Besides, I make a rotten alcoholic. I always get deathly ill when I've too much or am emotionally upset like Friday. I don't seem to get drunk except when I drink with people. Socially, I'm afraid. I drink. I lose a part of me. It probably isn't alcohol, but it helps.

I like to blame my mistakes on the booze. After all, I would be perfectly sober, but as I try sobriety and find I still make mistakes and am imperfect. There is nothing to blame except me. Hard. That's hard.

"Poppa, I think I'm gettin' high on feeling low."

I quit. I retire to the Little Death. The daily death—Sleep—though "Night won't set me free."

Love won't either but I want it to!

I'm going to mail this. And want it to be waiting for you when you get home.

Who cares?????

"I refuse to grow up until someone satisfies my needs!" wrote Nathaniel Branden.

Thursday

This is one of the longest weeks of my life and there is more to go yet.

Monday at 10:30 I have an appointment with the gynecologist. I didn't tell you but I may get my vacation in the hospital. He said he might have to do an exploratory D&C. He said most doctors, given my symptoms, would jerk out my womb, but he didn't believe in that, especially if I was having emotional problems already. You Bet! I always thought that it wouldn't bother me if I had to have it done, but can you imagine what taking my womanhood away would cost me now when I'm so uncertain of it?

Intellect couldn't rescue me from that either.

Monday, my father has an appointment with the psychiatrist. He says that's the day he is getting out. He'll be on his own again. God! It hurts me! It hurts me when my father calls the place a "penitentiary." He's getting so well I think he is coming out and then we'll have to move him again for the fifth time this year. We'll set him up in an apartment. I think I'll disown him like he disowned my brother. I'll absolve myself of any responsibility for him. (Where have I heard that before?) He could live to be ninety-six—twenty more years of this! Too bad one can't divorce one's parents.

One more thing. Jake made me angry. I did him, too, by not coming home until 6 a.m. He said, "Why didn't you call?" I didn't know what time it was until I looked at my watch at about 5 a.m. and by that time, he had already left for work, getting up at about 4 a.m. that day. Besides, I told him that I felt it might be a Freudian slip because of repressed anger—for twenty years, he hasn't called me when he works overtime! Endless ruined meals, missed social engagements, sometimes waiting till midnight or later, wondering, sort of, if he's working or dead someplace. No double standards.

Jake really made me angry after Thursday's Breakdown Day when he said words to the effect of, "In the future, when you break down, don't do it where the kids can see you. It disturbs them. You should have seen the look on Jill's face!"

What about me, People? What about me? I should avoid having a nervous breakdown because it disturbs other people!

Nobody, including me, ever thought of me as fragile before. That's lovely! Why do I have any right to hope anybody is going to be any different than anyone I've ever encountered before in my life?

Forget it, Jan.

You will anyway! I don't need you! Forget it and be healthy. You're not responsible for me. I am irresponsible—I am in danger.

Fuck you Sister!

Who Needs You!

I DO!

Jan on January 20, 1974

Dear Bea,

I don't know what to say.

Jan on February 5, 1974

Snow turned from flurries to cottony fluff piling into a deep comforter of wedding white as we watched it change through frosty Emerson House windows on Friday night. The billowy quilt covered the park across the street and all around as we gathered again for another TA marathon. Quiet and restful now with the wind moving on, clouds of goose-feather down revealed shadowed patterns of snow-weighted trees from the park lights that reflected sugar-crystal shining sparkles from Mother Nature's deep, pure, healing bed.

And here comes Bea back into our circle again and, being her unpredictable self, we held our breaths. Who were we to "let" her attend and who were we to feel responsible for others' psychological reactions in this intimate circle of persons with their individual issues? Emotionally edgy, she fascinates and bewitches me. Though I've experienced enough tension and uncertainty in my life, I was going to rescue Bea and make her feel good. I know what it is emotionally to love a woman and I know when that love is not returned.

Who do I think I am? Anyway, she's so intense. She represents all the scary thoughts that I had about my mother. Not that Bea's crazy, but my thoughts focus on her so often and I never know what she's going to do. Yes. I'm afraid that she might commit suicide. I fear that, yet I can't risk myself either way: to let her be or to try to stop her.

If Mother Nature's storm had been raging rather than at rest, the anxiety of the individuals may not have been contained. We worked on softer issues like our parents and relationships rather than confronting our personal battles.

When it was my turn, I spoke of my mother's life and how it may reflect on the decisions I'm making now. "You never stop loving your mother when you lose her as a child—even though, in my case, she is still alive."

I told my story that I was cesarean born to a sick mother mourning the recent loss of her eight-year-old son from her first marriage. He was killed when hit by a car. Many relatives always told me that I cried a lot as a baby. Those were the days of strict routines—before Dr. Spock gave mothers permission to respond naturally to their babies' needs. I must have been a lonely infant.

I talked Marge into going to the park to make angels in the snow. No one else wanted to go and she grumbled some, but when she stopped being an "adult" and let her "kid" play again, she had fun with me. It felt so good doing that when I was a child and with my kids when they were young. The air was clean, the snow so soft, we were refreshed.

Jan on February 7, 1974

I woke from my sleeping nest on the floor of Emerson House. I stood up to sit in the halo of a small desk lamp so as not to wake the rest. I still cared for Marge, especially with Bea so unstable. I wrote a note to Marge at 4 a.m., but I never gave it to her. She seldom answers anyway, which is her pattern in dealing with me. It read, "I need to know what you mean when you look at me and say, 'If I didn't have other reinforcements.' I need to know what you mean when someone else touches my shoulders and you talk to me with your eyes. What do you imply? What are you telling me? I need to know. God damn it! I need to know."

Bea and Betty were quiet during the evening session, but early the next morning, before the day's session started, Bea almost collapsed from tension and conflict. She lay on the carpet and sobbed her heart out. Several of us circled around her and we tried to give Bea support and show her that we cared for her. Before Saturday ended, Bea promised Rachael to try TA therapy for a couple of nights at Rachael's Milwaukee home.

Randy King was not at this session, thank goodness.

To reinforce her decision to get some therapy, Bea and I agreed to meet every Thursday afternoon to discuss our poetry and writing, but on Tuesday, she mailed a card saying, "Dear Jan, You don't owe me anything but I owe you something—your freedom from me. Let's forget Thursday. Love, Bea." However, she changed her mind and came to see me and we had a calm and pleasant afternoon together.

Bea read aloud Sidney Omar's current affirming horoscopes.

Bea's a Gemini. "Gemini is changeable, artistic, perceptive and often foolish. Gemini is flirtatious, affectionate and often falls in love with individuals who are not worthy. Gemini is intelligent and cannot easily be fooled. However, these natives can do a pretty good job of getting themselves in hot water, usually by not permitting logic to take over from impulse."

My Scorpio said, "Scorpio is intense, seldom accepting halfway measures, insisting on getting to the core, investigating, discovering modus operandi. Here is the detective, the surgeon, the individual with an insatiable curiosity who lives and loves to the hilt. Scorpio is active, creative, yearning, often impulsive and possessing qualities which are at once ingratiating and grating."

"Thanks for helping me make the most of my being a Scorpio," I quietly responded.

Jan on February 11, 1974

Something awesome yet scary happened last night. Bea, Marge, Anna, Betty and I went to a Theater Guild play, *The Effect of Gamma Rays on Man in the Moon Marigolds*, because a church friend was one of the major performers. The crowded little theater was close and hot. I had to laugh when Bea almost pushed our friends out of the way so she could sit next to me. During the play, we looked at each other and Bea and I actually felt electric shock waves crackling through us—and it wasn't static electricity from our clothing, nor was it the effect of gamma rays. Startled, we stared at each other, blood pressure rising, palpitations and the rush of experiencing this phenomenon. After the performance, I sat in the driver's seat and Bea lunged again in front of everyone to get into the center front seat next to me—and we heard a crackle and we felt the sparks again. You could almost see the electrical energy glow. I drove them to my house for wine and my lentil soup. Of course, I hugged everyone goodbye and Betty climbed in Bea's car and they all drove off.

Confused about my emotions, afraid of an unstable friend and bewildered by all these events, I woke at 4:15 a.m. and scrawled at my studio desk undelivered questions to Marge.

How do I protect myself from a love I do not desire,
yet get the touch I care to have?
Must I turn back on what I ache to have
because it's not from the one I want?
How can I protect myself?
How long can I resist
what I get from another, but not from you?

Bea on February 11, 1974

I called Jan as soon as I knew Alex and the kids would be gone and before she went to work. "Holy mackerel, I feel like I'm hungover; I must learn better control and am feeling awfully Not OK. But I had to talk with you about those electric sparks that flew between us. That's never happened to me. How about you?"

"I don't think so."
"Please, your voice is sending more shock waves. This is stunning. And if you want to be stunned again, come with me to my first TA session tonight with Rachael.
"Good luck. I have to go now. I'll call you soon."

Jan on February 11, 1974

Those sparks ticked off a memory of my college artist friend Maria Grassi with her long black hair and striking, bold features. She lived in the dorm too and walked about her unit naked like a life model in one of her classes. I admired her courage to be natural about her body and I may have adopted her example, but my room next to the lobby door and my windows at street level made me more cautious.

Maria's art was progressing as she continued on to earn a master's degree. She'd moved out of the dorm and into a mini apartment that she decorated with her painting, several sculpture pieces, wall hangings, and lots of color. I called to ask to stop by and say farewell before she was to leave Madison for Italy to continue studying art. She moved like a cat across the room and served tea and Italian cookies on a decorated tray. In fact, she showed me how her cat would sit on the phonograph turntable and spin. Dressed in a long black gown, her feet were bare but she wore Moroccan ankle bracelets adorned with tiny brass bells. Her hair and eyes and eyebrows seemed blacker than usual, but her broad lips lined with vivid red lipstick confirmed that she was genuinely pleased to see me as we sat on her wicker settee.

"How's married life?"

"How's single life?" and we laughed knowing that she probably was getting as much sex as I was.

She turned away to reach the cookie plate and offer me more and when she faced me again, I experienced a rushing electric spark that made me forget where I was, a white light, a flash of body heat. And I awkwardly backed away from my free-spirited friend, and tried to catch my breath before my stunned reaction could be noticed.

"Wow! That felt good!" I remembered, *"What was happening to me then—at that point in my life?"*

We said our goodbyes, wished each other wonderful successes, and I didn't see Maria for three or four years. She returned from Italy with an infant son, Peter, and an Italian husband to begin her new life in San Francisco.

Bea on February 18, 1974

I found Rachael's house okay but I was afraid and that was only the beginning of these sessions. One of the kids in the group talked about wanting to be able to cry because it seemed she had a block about that. Rachael asked her to ask each of us what it was we cried for when we did. People answered with stories about sadness, when someone dies, happiness and so on.

I said, "I never used to cry much. I always held that back. I used to cry at a sad movie. They'd hook me every time. Crying like mad over unreality—but not reality.

"I never cried over my mother's death. My friend Angie knew it and remarked about it one day. She knew how deeply I did feel because I couldn't go near the cemetery where my mother was buried. About a year later, I locked myself in my room and bawled my head off for about two hours. And finally, in the past three months, I've done more crying than I ever had in my life. Reality. Unreality. Have I actually thrown away my book of guilt stamps? Or is it almost ready to be cashed out?"

I didn't tell them that I never cried over my brother's death. When I heard they had found him, I hung up the phone, walked into the living room, sat on the hassock and said, 'That poor son of a bitch.' And my father, my aunt and uncle, Jake and I laughed and joked on the way to his pathetic funeral service before his cremation.

I tried to put an end to what was wrong by their standards. Are they afraid of my individuality? They told me pleasure was wrong, tasting life was wrong, and feeling was wrong. Why? Why should I let them when I've done nothing wrong? My joy is pure and clean and vibrant and alive. My "me" is unique—imperfect, perhaps by their standards, but not, by God, by mine.

Jan on February 27, 1974

Our Thursday afternoons have turned into tender, romantic, creative interludes with poetry and music, conversation and polite affection with delightful sexual tension minus any moves toward physical gratification. I know that sounds corny, but it's true. When we meet at her house, at mine, in our cars, or in a park, we simultaneously burst forth to share our thoughts on each one's activities. We express feelings freely about the week's events and people without weighing or judging what we'd say or its impact. We're two open, honest, spontaneous women willing to trust each other. Sometimes we cry; most often, we laugh. We exchange details that would have ordinarily been overlooked. We remember colors, sounds, shapes and settings that would bore others, but to us, these details are vital ingredients in this new experience of being mutually creative.

Alex asked me one evening, "What are you smiling about?" My preoccupied mind was jarred and I said, "Oh, something funny happened," and I dredged up a story from a remote memory cell, any story to tell that was received with a casual response and we both returned to reading or watching TV.

Jan on February 27, 1974

Alex and I took Matt and Jenny to the Milwaukee Rep to see *Our Town* by Thornton Wilder, a play that made me appreciate life even more than before. I was so moved when Emily realizes after she dies that she's missed the joyful aspects of daily life.

In the cemetery scene at the end of the play, Emily says:
"...Oh earth, you are too wonderful for anybody to realize you. (She looks toward the stage manager and asks abruptly through her tears.) Do human beings ever realize life while they live it? — every, every minute?"
Stage Manager: "No." (Pause) "The saints and poets, maybe they do some."

CHAPTER ELEVEN

Bea on March 3, 1974

What a beautiful Sunday starting with a guest minister and his sermon, "Make a Joyful Noise." We were invited to read joyful poems and the whole program was perfect. I guess he's auditioning for our empty pulpit. We're enjoying the chance to do our own services, so we're not in any hurry to find a new minister. Besides, Alex is on the search committee that frequently takes him out of town on Sundays, leaving time for Jan and me when we're not busy with our kids.

I received two Edna St. Vincent Millay poems from her. Jan wrote little notes, "Something to share" and "Love" on the typed copy of the long *Renascence* and a poem starting with "Night is my sister and how deep in love, how weedily washed ashore" with many verses underlined, my favorites are

> "And as I looked a quickening gust
> Of wind blew up to me and thrust
> Into my face a miracle
> Of orchard-breath and with the smell,—
> I know not how such things can be!—
> I breathed my soul back into me."

and

> "No man will leave his friendly fire and snug
> For a drowned woman's sake and bring her back
> To drip and scatter shells upon the rug.
> No one but Night, with tears on her dark face,
> Watches beside me in this windy place."

I brought them with me when we met this afternoon at Pritchard Park. I was already waiting when she parked and joined me. This is where we met years ago with our Sunday school teaching friends and kids! An incredible sense of unreality persists. The feeling that I'm being directed somehow. Obsessed? Parallel lives? Parallel disasters?

These terrors changed to excitement as I watched her coming to me, waiting for her. She embraced me in the car that I inherited from my mother. I cried again—still shaky despite the warm sweetness of spring's soft sun melting winter and my mother's essence from this car. "I thanked my mailman who comes so early every day." I said, "I needed the mail that came today."

Jan answered, "I envy you. I have to wait until the afternoon for mine. That intrigues me because I wait to see if I get mail from you."

"God, those two Millay poems were beautiful, more so l than anything I've read in years."

"I'll keep on tantalizing you with Edna's poems when I can't think of anything to say. Hey, that sounds like that Cat Stevens' song."

"Helen Reddy. Keeps me going—inspiring me to write my own songs."

Jan said she loved my new musk-oil fragrance. She brushed my hair back from the side of my face, and put hers closer to my cheek and ear to inhale its primal scent. My stomach groaned, muscles tugged and pulled at my heart. I turned my face to hers and we kissed so gently, then with more fervor as we lost more of our inhibitions. We found the courage to caress each other's faces, to study the tactile interchanging of our hands and fingers exploring connections and to hold each other while we whispered romantic verses, songs and feelings.

"'Hey! Hey,' sings Helen Reddy, 'By the way! Thanks for giving me a little lovin',"" and then I realized, "What if a cop comes by?"

Jan boldly uttered as if she had rehearsed this statement, "My friend is sad. Can't I comfort my friend?"

We were preadolescents again learning how to touch, not yet desperate to move on—especially married women with teenage children. After two hours of surprisingly romantic and delightfully innocent affection for two women with our experience, especially mine, she announced that we needed some physical nourishment and she directed my weakened self to drive a few blocks to get a sandwich. We drove into the Cal's Roast Beef lot and parked.

Perhaps I am following my script. Speaking of risks! My brother Cal committed suicide because of what he was and we go to Cal's Roast Beef for lunch—of all places! Every time I see one of those restaurants, I remember that I saw them on television news, recovering his body from Lake Michigan. I couldn't stop myself from watching. There he was, floating face down and they were pulling at him with a boat hook.

I think it was while he was in the service that he began to question his sexual orientation. After coming home, Cal moved to New York to sample the big city life by hanging out in Greenwich Village with summers spent on Fire Island. I went to stay with him in New York for a week and he showed me the best of the Big Apple—and was discreet about his friends.

He must have suffered as a homosexual. He had been in and out of several mental hospitals, including New York's Bellevue, and he returned to live and work in Chicago. I don't know all that transpired, but when Calvin told our parents that he was gay, my dad disowned him and my mom went into the hospital with a nervous breakdown.

Perhaps Mom was remembering the pain she'd endured for years after she and their friends, who helped them build their Door County cabin, moved drunken Ducky from behind the wheel on their way back to their cabin after dining out. Mom took over driving the car with Ducky passed out in the front seat with the Nopenzs riding in the back. In the late twilight of the early summer night, a young boy darted out from the hedges along the road and ran directly in front of their sedan. She put on the brakes and swerved, but the 14-year-old boy was hit. His body went over the hood and got slammed against the support of the car's windshield visor and flipped over the back of the car. He was DOA at the hospital. The authorities did not arrest her. It was "just an accident" she had to live with for the rest of her life.

During her three months of treatment, she was given electroshock treatments. But there were bigger shocks when she came out of the hospital. In addition to disowning their son, my father had retired, sold the home they built in Park Ridge, and bought a house he picked in Southport, where he took her from the hospital to the Southport house and proudly installed her. He had uprooted her from all her Chicago friends, her organizations and circles. He even had my mother's remaining three cocker spaniels put down. He said he got mad at them when he stepped out of bed one morning and put his bare foot in a pile of dog shit. At least their new home was in Southport, where I lived with my husband and four kids.

When my father disowned Cal after he told them he was a homosexual, I wonder if he recalled what my mother always told us:

"You go jump in the lake."

On March 19, 1962, Calvin, 43, left his wristwatch on top of his dresser in his apartment and walked into Lake Michigan off the Gold Coast beach at Chicago's Outer Drive. Before that however, he called a telephone operator and said, "I need help."

She transferred Cal to me with my four kids, ages 7, 6, 4, and 3, all sick with chickenpox. He told me he was gay, that he'd told our parents, that our mother was having a mental breakdown, and that our father had disowned him. My brother and I talked on the phone for three hours.

I was the last person in the family to talk with him.

A month later, a Chicago TV newsman called me, told me to watch the night's news, and then called me back for my reaction to my brother Cal being fished out of Lake Michigan. I did see it on the news. I don't remember what I said to that bastard.

What could I have done? I was in Southport. I had to take care of my four sick children.

But my mom survived. She even thrived and joined Southport's First Methodist Church, its women's circle, and the Garden Club.

She made many more friends and avidly continued her craft fair activities, especially for the Christmas fair that she organized each year. Her house was filled with Christmas all year long.

Jan on March 7, 1974

At our weekly "poetry reading" this Thursday afternoon at my home, Bea sat on the slightly frayed yellow armchair next to me on the sofa.

Slivers of silver sunlight off Michigan's Lake rippling surface danced behind me. Bea's long hair and bravado black style, her slimming body shirt with a slight turtleneck collar, bell-bottom pants, her silver scalloped belt slung right above her hips and her leather boots made her appear as if she were a potential pirate or a roving troubadour. She brought her guitar and strummed some chords and sang a song she'd worked out. She took off her silver-rimmed blue sunglasses and handed me the lyrics typed with the preface:

> Let's not sublimate in poems
> what we can celebrate in song
> And Helen Reddy sings:
> "First thing in the morning, I make a pot of tea
> Then I have the morning whistling songs back at me.
> I do a little tap dance to a cracked-up 33....
> Thanks for givin' me a little lovin'."

And then Bea sang her song to me.

> "Words"
> I can't tell you how much I love you
> because it can't be said in words.
> From across the room, I love you silently,
> my eyes speak things I cannot say.
> I can't tell you how much I love you
> because the words get in the way

Chorus:

Words. Weak little words. Words that I can say.
Words. Let me say words, words that sound okay.

I can't tell you how much I love you
because it can't be said in words.
I can only hold you close to me
and hope you read it in my touch.
When we meet like this,
I hunger for your kiss, but
I know I will not say,
I can't tell you how much I love you
because the words get in the way.

So I can tell you, at last, I love you
and how much I need your tender touch.
And how I want you so much
and how I want you so much.

When she put down her guitar, I held out my arms to have her join me on our soft sofa pillows. I gave her a hug and a harmless, gratuitous kiss.

"Thanks," she said, "You're welcome. I'm glad you like it. I tried to make a tape of it but it was such a hassle with people coming in and out and the dog barking. It only adds to the situation that I'm so—what's the word? Frustrated. I even wear dark glasses to hide how much I've cried, how much I cry now."

"I'm so sorry that you're feeling so depressed," and I put my arm around her shoulder.

"It's not depression. It's frustration because I can't express what my emotions scream to say. My wants, my needs, and my desires are frustrated at every turn by people like you who care yet are scared because we think we know where our friendship is leading. Plus circumstances box me in on all sides by people who couldn't care less, like people who need me like all my kids' friends around all day and night, by people who love me like my kids who want me to do everything for them and maybe even people who hate me."

"No one hates you, Bea," and I gave her a gentle hug. "You're too intelligent and captivating for that to happen."

"Ha! My husband barely tolerates me. It's not enough for me to have sex once a year, like on my birthday. But most of all, he's not interested in anything that has value to me and inside I groan with the pain of being unfulfilled."

"Oh, my dear Bea—"

She turned to me with tears, yet with strength and as if calling out to the universe, she closed her eyes and uttered, "Make room for me, people! Make way. I must have what I need or I'll split wide open!"

And in trying to release my friend's frustrated passion, we went beyond the boundaries that we'd set for ourselves: to foster each other's creativity, enthusiasm and accomplishments. With my simple, adolescent and unskilled execution—and our being fully clothed, I moved beyond our unspoken but understood limits and I tried to release her tension with my affection. We surrendered to our suppressed passions in a whirl of movement that united our full length on the softness of the sofa pillows. My intent was to free her, to release her of her emotional pain by giving her the gift of satisfaction.

Encircling her slight body completely with my arms around her shoulders, I felt new power to initiate tenderness without overpowering her beneath me. We were equals as her arms held on to me as if she would fall away should she let go. Our smiling faces, velvety cheeks—without whiskers or stubble—a woman's scent and warmth, lips so supple and responding in kind to mine, the taste of her lipstick. Her neck, ears and under her chin were sanctuaries as my lips, my mouth, and my breath found sweet refuge in her silken skin. I found the strength to hold on, the courage to respond, the excitement of friction from fully clothed bodies, our thighs and loins. My hands traveled from her back to her slim hips. I was committed to moving and pressing her even closer to release her passion.

With shocking surprise for both of us, I was amazed at experiencing my first overwhelming orgasmic release with a woman— with Bea! In its lingering duration, I stammered loudly, "Oh Matt! Don't come—home—from school now!"

We were both stunned. Shock! Trauma! Laughter! Joyful exhaustion! A puzzle: I was not the one deprived of sexual fulfillment!

Why should it be me?

She drew my mouth softly to hers and kissed me gently.

"What happened?" I asked dumbly.

"That's enough for now, dear. We don't want to set this sofa on fire, yet."

We stopped and unraveled ourselves from each other. I struggled to reorganize my thoughts and staggered to the kitchen to fix us a drink.

Her brown eyes lined with blue stared at me over the glass I offered her; her hand holding a cigarette with its spiraling smoke melting me. Her raised eyebrow sparked a memory from the past with a Lauren Bacall voice saying in my mind, "If you want me, just whistle. You know how to whistle, don't you? You just put your lips together and blow."

When Bea left me and drove away to pick up her kids at school, I could barely walk to the window to watch her. I returned to that sofa scene with my body and senses still vibrating and let out a long, slow, quiet whistle and dozed off until my son came in the back door and opened the refrigerator.

Jan on March 8, 1974

I mailed her more poems, trying to explain, redeem, and cool down. In a folded testimonial, so carefully composed, I placed a white feather with this verse.

> Subdued by power beyond his strength,
> he lost control and dropped his guard.
> The day the Cavalier caved in—
> collapsed by stronger weapons of tender touch—
> was sweet surrender to love and peace.
>
> Bruised within, he wears no scars
> to show the conflict he survived—
> except a vacant glance upon the scene
> as his heart recalls the battle anthem
> and his mind creates a phrase
> to turn surrender into song.

> A call to rapier arms no more,
> yet he can still wear a white plume.
> March 7, 1974

On another sheet, I wrote:

> There is no hurry to test the hardness
> of this new power that we've discovered.
> It would be better perhaps, to nurture so tenderly
> the delicate beginnings of a new being growing
> from so frail a start in such fragile ground,
> subject to storms and elements beyond our control
> that can ruin its critical early life.
>
> Impatient and eager to know what we have
> and penetrate to its core to uncover its potential,
> we must softly and gracefully handle it with care
> this uncertain force with its new dimension.
>
> There is no hurry. This power will live.
> We've got time to understand.
> We'll find space for the power to grow.
> There is no hurry.
>
> Too fast, too desperate perhaps to fill
> the too-long empty needs of two people
> who live gracefully
> March 7, 1974

Bea on March 12, 1974

Jan sent me this poem. I don't know where I stand with her—or anyone. Why does this always happen to me? Does she think that she was only trying to help me?

Jan wrote:

> I "rescued" a friend from having to choose
> which of the feelings this person should use.
> Her "Why do you hurt me?" exploded my reason,
> releasing compassion I thought I controlled.

Both of us empty, I plunged into the void
filling my own needs with self-serving fervor.
Both of us hurting, now accepted as equals,
years of frustration swept clear by release.
It was good to be held by one loving me fully.
Then tenderness turned to more heated emotions.

I hung on—to passion. I could not contain it;
 would not, perhaps; did not, for certain.
I wanted to tame it, to put it at rest; but
to exorcise passion is not my profession.
Amateur! Stupid! I bungled along
ineffectually responding to one so strong.
I lost my control, then overreacted,
attempting to meet the needs of my friend.

A forced decision to halt this behavior
 brought quiet intensity to the scene.
Tenderly talking of intimate feelings
of trust and of love made affections profound.
We're stronger now, wiser, mature in our knowing
 the range of our feelings, the depth of our needs.
And the choice of our actions for now and in the future
will be strengthened, enhanced,
by perceptions we've gained.

Why am I prone to courting these feelings?
Someday my rescuer may come along—
Jan

CHAPTER TWELVE

Bea on March 17, 1974

What a crazy night on Friday! I'm still recovering. First folk dancing, then to Shannon's afterward for singing in front of the fireplace, then a sauna. It was raining, then snowing. I don't know why, but that wine gets to me faster than others. And that Pete gets to me too. The two of us went outside after the sauna and Pete said he'd like to make an angel in the snow. Ha! Me!

Eventually, I followed Marge home in my car in the storm and when she invited me in for some coffee, I took her up on her invitation. Regrettably for her, I kept her up talking all night and I didn't get home until 7:30 a.m.

I had a lot to talk to her about. Of course, that damn Pete was smug about having me, but I was devastated afterward. I had been faithful to Jake since we met and married and I let that fuzzy-faced bastard finally have me, or should I say, I had him. No wonder I got so sick again at Marge's and threw up. This business with Pete and the sauna. It was something I had to do. To find out if sex had anything to do with what was lacking in my life. But a sex affair is nothing. You can have sex with a bedpost. Without caring, understanding, deep feelings, and empathy, without locking minds with someone as well as bodies, sex is empty.

In the process, that's when I told Marge that I knew that Jan loved her but Marge gave her friendship in return—agape love. "That's fine for nuns and martyrs, but she's not either," I said. "Jan has a lot of love to give and she deserves to get what she needs in return."

"Well, if she'd pay attention to how lucky she is," Marge chided, "she'd be a contented person. For Christ's sake, she's got everything anyone would want."

"I've told her to go back to her husband and family so many times and she keeps sending me all these poems and shows such deep affection for me, affection as I've never had before." I sucked in extra oxygen and told Marge, "I love Jan so much I can barely breathe when I think of her and I can't think straight either—when we're together— and when we're apart.

Marge said she couldn't get involved in a relationship with a woman. She's had other women friends who wanted to, but even though she cares for Jan as her sister and friend, she is strictly male-oriented, "and I don't want to mess up my life being, of all things, a lesbian."

"Marge. Tell me that you definitely do not want her."

"Bea! I do not want Jan that way!"

"OK then. I'll try my best to be the one for her. I hope you'll still be my friend. I know you'll be discreet about this and keep it a secret. I hope I can work through all the conflicts and chaos. I need a friend like you, Marge. Thank you for taking care of me. I know I've been a handful at times and you've always come through for me.

Thank you."

Jan on March 20, 1974

Marge called me, "Don't do anything until I talk with you. I'll see you at your house."

"Come for breakfast at 8:30."

Of course, I was curious, but busy too with work deadlines and kids and the house. I called Bea, but she'd groan and say she had too much medicine over the weekend.

Bea did mail me this poem with this note:

> If it's downhill all the way
> from a midpoint in your life, that's terrific!
> Because now you can coast
> with the exhilaration of movement,
> with the joy of being alive.
>
> And—while you're busy balancing your life to fit me in,
> I keep falling off my tight rope!
> Bea

Marge came promptly for breakfast and directly began to tell me graphic details about Bea and Pete's bawdy indiscretions on Friday night, how again she had to get Bea sobered up before she would let her finally drive to Southport at dawn and how she had to listen again to all her problems and conflicting remedies.

"But most of all, Jan, she told me more details about what you two are up to. Do you realize how dangerous this is and what this will do to you, your marriage and your children if this comes out in the open, exposed?"

"It's easy for you to judge. You can't understand how long I've repressed these feelings and yet how terrified I am of them—and afraid of Bea's behavior too and yet I love the excitement of it all."

"It will probably be her behavior that will cause you to lose all that you have. Sure, she's exciting and fun to be with, but there are limits and good judgment as to what you say and where."

"I guess I want to remember only the good stuff."

"She actually asked me if I wanted you, as if you were a slave."

"What did you say?"

"You know how I feel about our friendship. I, of course, said not in that way did I want you. Then she said that if I didn't want you, she would get you—as if you were a piece of meat to buy."

"Her dramatic flair is only one aspect of her personality. She's different when she's with me. She can be so loving and tender and vulnerable, as am I. We know each other and knowing more is so important to me—and to her, even if we're both afraid of the consequences." Of course, I started to cry. "Maybe that's why we experience such electricity when we're together."

"You have to divorce her, Jan, before it's too late!"

The ringing phone jolted both of us. I slowly went over to pick up the receiver. It was Bea's voice and I almost died of shock.

"Hi, Babe!" she blustered as if to gloss over her nervousness. "When can I see you again? Soon, I hope. I have a lot to tell you. I've been in a vulnerable place again but I feel stronger now."

Marge picked up my signal that it was Bea on the phone and she came next to me, holding me in her arms, her ear next to mine to hear Bea's voice. I didn't notice then, but that was the first time Marge had truly held me. My mind and heart were struggling with the painful words I needed to say and how I was to respond. "I'm sorry, but I don't feel very strong right now," and my rib cage seemed to fall into my weary chest. I couldn't sit down because Marge was, in effect, holding me up.

What a strange triangle we were: three friends, church school teachers, buddies, almost sisters who were so close and could exchange confidences and intimate details of our lives. Three women friends recovering together from dissolving or disappearing marriages: three women, eight kids, two part-time jobs and two husbands who could perhaps be joining the third in the ex-husband status of family life.

"Jan," Bea whispered, "I love you!"

"I know, Bea, but I can't be loving to you anymore. I'm so sorry, but I can't," I choked. "Maybe we can talk again when things cool down between us, but I don't know when and I can't explain why."

"Goodbye then?"

"Yes. Goodbye, Bea." I hung up and turned to Marge in grief from my loss. She let me go and I crumpled in the chair next to the phone and stared, wondering what I had done.

I promised myself that I would never—could never see Bea again because of my fear of her and of our emotions. I could not accept her love and we could not exist together under these pressures. I cannot risk loving anyone who is not in control. Perhaps the euphoria that I felt was "An exaggerated state of well-being." No matter how—it's gone. Life's back to normal now.

Bea on March 20, 1974

Rejection! Again! I finally generated the nerve to call her and I got rejected! After I slammed the phone down, I slumped into the nearest soft chair to get my mind back in gear. She must have heard about Friday night and now she thinks I'm too unstable for her. Damn!

The door opened and in walked one of the teens who emotionally clings to me, who haunts me with problems and asks me for advice when I can't even take care of myself. I've had it. I'm getting away. I'll give Jake the choice when he gets home from work. I'm going to the hospital or to a motel for a couple of days.

Did you ever try to hit a tennis ball with your eyes full of tears and your body shuddering with the tremendous emotion of total grief? I'm alone with my tennis wall—alone, with no human being to play against. No matter how hard I hit the ball, it will not go through the wall. The wall is a wall that walls me in—in my loneliness. Jan has Alex and Marge, even Rachael. I accept no one. I stand alone and the tears run down my face as I run and hit the ball against the wall. The wall that walls me into myself. The wall that I tried to climb, but merely peeked through, found a hole and actually touched someone through that hole. But my touch burned and seared that person, nearly destroyed her. Close up the wall. Hit tennis balls against the wall of loneliness. It will never be breached again. I'm going to be the first woman to cross the Pacific alone and my journey starts now.

When one dies in battle, it's best that the best, most intelligent and most heroic of warriors be the instrument of his destruction. A lot of me has died in battle with you. I've learned much about human relations. I've learned that life is a do-it-yourself project. I've learned that there is only one God, me; the God who lives within—Self Reliance.

CHAPTER THIRTEEN

Bea on March 21, 1974

I have a bruise in the middle of my forehead where I brained myself on the steering wheel last night while having one of the tremendous crying jags of my life—and now I'm here in Two Rivers at the Waveside Inn on Lake Michigan, my lake! I need time alone and I never get it anymore, ever. To be able to fight again, to sail the sea of storms, I must rest and it was a choice of here or in the hospital. I like here better; it's luxurious.

From the swimming pool windows, I see spray leaping into the air from the waves crashing against rocks not five feet from the motel wall. And I float and bob aimlessly in their pool, warm inside as a white seagull soars gently and gracefully past the window. I shower, wash my hair, run gallons and gallons of water and shudder through an extraordinary orgasm.

I'm going to enjoy while I can—think, read, write and try to forget the most colossal love of my life and perhaps the most foolish. I'm also going to be more honest than I've ever been with myself and with anyone who gives a damn enough to read this someday. I don't care anymore what's right or wrong. I must tell it like it is—at long last. Maybe that way, I'll quit kidding myself as well.

When there's nothing left of the life that mattered for twenty years, love is offered—complete with understanding, and empathy— a love that is the kind of love you want because a woman who yearns for it too can give it from the yearning that she has. I know how to kiss, stroke, hold, and love in the way I want to be kissed, stroked, held and loved—in a way I'd never been; yet, I've always wanted it.

A love that has to do with ancient yearnings for mother, with a desire to return to the womb where all was safe and comfortable.

And it turned me on so intensely that I thought of nothing else. I was stoned in love. I couldn't eat, sleep, concentrate—my body ached for her from head to toe. My child inside cried and it cried when I had to leave her or when I needed and wanted her. I never cried so much or so hard in my life as I have since November when this all started. I cherished everything about her, but especially her intelligence, warmth and wit.

Skyrockets when off inside me when I saw her—and when I thought of her. I was totally, insanely, madly in love with her. I'd never been in love like that before and suddenly, I knew what all the poets were saying, what everyone had ever said about real love. And all the while, I was in turmoil because this love was for another woman.

I tried to end the relationship a dozen times, in a dozen different ways, but each time she came back with love and caring and I couldn't go through with it. I wanted her more and more, even when I knew how impossible it was.

And she was so damn confusing. First, she would suggest, "What could it hurt if we just let it happen," and then she would say, "I can't," when I only wanted to hold her, nothing more. And after our most torrid encounter, she told me we could make it work—we could make a possibility of it in between our lives' inanities, while I kept saying how impossible it was.

And then suddenly, SLAM! She put her adult in gear at last and declared, "I can't" again. This time finally.

It broke me into shards.

I shook her to her core. I made her "risk all that she is" for me. But I risked it, too. An incredible love. Higher than the sky. I wonder if I'll ever find it again.

I'm so coldly rational right now. I guess it's because I'm so damn tired, emotionally worn to a frazzle. I felt every emotion in the book these past months and so damn intense. I shook. I trembled. Because joyously euphoric, I cried. I moaned. I screamed. I laughed to high heaven. I was violently passionate. I was impulsive, so impulsive I kissed strange men and hugged strange women.

I knew all along it couldn't be, but I kept wanting it. Such an incredible feeling. Such intensity. "A woman in love is temporarily out of her mind," wrote Simone de Beauvoir in *The Second Sex*.

Jan on March 24, 1974

Bea missed Sunday's service, but she made it for coffee hour at our church, where we had met almost ten years ago when we were Sunday school teachers raising our children. Now she stood, detached and calm, looking at me through ice-blue sunglasses. She showed me she did not need me to rescue her. Yet we did need to talk.

Perhaps I needed her to rescue me from the shock of knowing I had lost the one person who accepted me as I was, who loved me completely.

We went for brunch and talked rationally about our past months of chaotic emotional binges.

"I was really worried about you all these days and tried to concentrate on what was going on at work and home. It wasn't completely successful, however, at getting you out of my mind."

Bea explained that she had to have time to think. "I swam and wrote and tried to rest. When I stopped at Two Rivers on Thursday night, I decided to stay there rather than drive to Door County. I had a lovely supper with a small bottle of champagne—and I slept. Keep in charge. I didn't want to cry again. My eyes were terribly swollen."

"I'm sorry you were so shaken up. I'm truly sorry I had to hurt you."

"Well, I knew all along we couldn't be together, but I kept wanting those incredible feelings with such intensity. I knew you had to do what you did—my mother surrogate," she said softly but added with a sharper note as she leaned back against the chair, "Like my mother would say, 'Get lost. You go jump in the lake.' My brother's script, somewhat like mine that he followed to his death. But Jan, I am not my brother!"

"Did it seem like a long time to be alone? Were you lonesome?"

"Ha! One night after watching Carol Burnett on TV in my room, I decided to go down to the bar for a couple of brandy old fashions. What the hell! I'm me, remember? I walked into the crowded bar, two people left their seats and I took one. A few minutes later, a guy walked in. Six-foot four. Bearded. Terribly attractive. And he sat next to me. He had an English accent. I could feel my pulse racing. Gods. I am human, I thought."

"Of course you are and at your prime. Don't tell me you went to bed with him?"

"No! Is that a dig at me?"

"No! I was only kidding you. But he must have been a faithful married man or else he was gay."

But what a surprise! He talked to the bartenders in that lovely accent. The bartender asked, "Growing a beard? Tell you what you do. Soak it in beer every night. Then one night, don't and the beard will come out looking for it." I laughed with them.

"A few minutes went by before I experienced a terrific blast of ESP. When we began to talk, I thought, 'I know him. He is all the Englishmen I had ever read about. Intelligent. Adventurous. He'd been everywhere in the world. Venice. New Zealand. Canada. All over the States. And damned, if he bloody well wasn't a small boat sailor. I don't remember it all, but he talked beautifully about his adventurous life, sailing 15-footers in England and Scotland, and crewing on a 27-footer. I traded some stories with him too. We talked boats—and diving and God knows what else. If I hadn't gone down there, if I hadn't had to guts enough to do it—alone, I would have missed that. Salute to Life! Salute to the future! I'm a winner. I may sail the Pacific yet."

Sitting at the bar, we saluted each other with our drinks and walked to the small table set for our lunch.

"Only you would think of sailing the Pacific, Bea. When are you in snow-bound Two Rivers?"

"Can you image me, the shivering one, walking in a snowstorm, a blizzard—and I stayed warm! The snow was so thick that it fell in my eyes, so I couldn't see. I wanted to walk along the beach, but the storm prevented that, so I headed for civilization and back through the town. I sense a heavy scent in the air, strong yet pleasant, like hot sawdust or scorched hardwood. I went back to the cocktail lounge, where I felt as if I were on a boat with the magnificent lake right outside the window. Snow tumbled down outside, obscured the horizon and inside, the water dripped from my forehead from the melting snow in my hair."

"What a cleansing experience for you, Bea."

"Jan, I wonder if I can tell you—," she leaned forward, "how many times I tried to break off our relationship. But I never could go through with it. I sensed you didn't want me to, how you wanted this romantic love—and needed it. I couldn't break it off because I knew I might hurt you more by stopping than by continuing.

"Bea, do you think I project homo-emotional messages?"

"You do! Yes, you do. And I picked up your signals. Then everything changed suddenly and I felt the first landslide of emotion. I had to get away from you. Remember? I said, 'I don't want this. I don't want a damn sex scene.' And it was you who said, 'What could it hurt?'"

"But I only kissed you."

"Ha! You were so shaken you don't even remember, do you? Then I said, 'It could hurt you and it could hurt me. You're not strong enough for this and neither am I.' And it's obvious that I'm right!

Bea tipped up her glass to get the last drop of brandy. "You know what? In the TA session I went to at Rachael's place, someone said her husband gave her nothing and Rachael asked her if she ever got her strokes from women? Sure, in the group it was perfectly all right for a 'loving couple' of two normal, girl-women to stroke and hug and love one another, almost in ecstasy, for nearly half an hour. This happened during my second and last session in Milwaukee and I began this session by saying that my biggest problem was that I had gotten myself emotionally involved with another woman. And Rachael responded, "Everyone is bisexual. So what else is new?"

The waitress came with our sandwiches and we didn't speak until she left. We had the dining room all to ourselves.

"In reality, Bea," I said softly, "I wouldn't have missed what we've experienced that showed me heights I never dreamed of and depths I never thought I could break through and still survive."

"And I have survived," said Bea, "and now I shine like burnished silver because I've been polished by it all."

"You always speak in such poetic verse."

"Poetry, no less. I've always disliked poetry—because of its impracticability, because of the hopeless market for it."

"But suddenly we're both poets," I proclaimed, "and you with songs, lyrics and music springing out of you."

"Yes. But a poem is but a tiny, crystallized thought. For someone like me who values the novel form, it's a bit of a cop-out. A quick masturbatory orgasm. A quickie screw. The novel is infinitely drawn out and slowly manipulated, growing directly to a bursting climatic orgasmic love act."

She looked around to see if anyone could hear her. "Something like my feelings about us. I don't need any orgasm. I feel the skyrockets bursting in my body going on and on, every synapse, every neuron in my body connecting and electrifying my total being. I could light up like a Christmas tree. I'm sure my aura glows and crackles. The feelings alone are like one giant, shattering, shuddering orgasm going on and on forever. It's beautiful. The pressure, the tremendous tension."

"Please. Keep telling me. I'm trying to remember everything you say. And I relive it while I'm writing."

"We're both good writers. I simply haven't been in the right place at the right time with the right stuff. I may never be, but when I try to stop writing, to bottle myself up, I end up bursting out of the weirdest directions. And I'm a good teacher, too. But my college degree and fifteen cents will get me a cup of coffee—anywhere. I've always considered myself a natural teacher."

"You are a natural at whatever you set your mind to do, Bea. But I must tell you this. Marge was with me when you called. She told me about that Friday night with Pete and you and she told me to divorce you. I'm embarrassed to tell you, but she was even listening to your voice by coming close so she could hear."

"I figured she had a lot to do with your decision."

"But I don't think I can go through this all again. And I hope most of all that we can still be friends."

"We can still be friends. We will be. We are so much a part of each other now. After we both cool off a little—if that is possible—we will keep a beautiful, deep friendship. Don't feel bad because you have to be the strong one. I know you try to help with love and I believe you're incapable of loving only one person. Are you afraid you'll be abandoned and hurt? I don't know. Perhaps that's why you spread yourself around to have so many people to care for."

We both declined when the waitress asked if we wanted any dessert and only asked for the check.

We understood—I understood the two of us better than I had before. We'd reached an agreement to be only good friends but after a cooling-off period. And when we parted, I had the nerve to give her my journal to read—a justification of myself and my actions.

CHAPTER FOURTEEN

Bea on March 25, 1974

I'm back and my life is the same. And I'm stealing these few moments alone for myself in my bedroom, where I've dumped all the sewing junk on the desk, tossed the bills aside, slung the sewing machine to the other side of the room and dusted off space for my typewriter and my mind. One of my kids' friends plays my guitar and another sings just beyond my open door. It would be a waste of time to shut it. They never respect closed doors anyway.

No one missed me much while I was in Two Rivers, except perhaps Jill who had all my responsibilities, but she was not taking it lying down. She mobilized them all to help. God, that kid has potential. She even had Jake washing the dishes, something he's never done for me in twenty years of marriage.

I always said I'd be replaced and by better help.

I read Jan's "journal" twice already—once last night and again this morning. At first reading, I thought metaphorically of a matchstick puzzle. You know, "Here are seven matches, can you make a square out of them by only moving two?" I was really hurt again when it seemed that she used me as the villain, her *Witch Wife*, another poem by Edna. "

She has more hair than she needs; In the sun 'tis woe to me!"

"She loves me all that she can,

And her ways to my ways resign;
But she was not made for any man,
And she never will be all mine.

But when I read it again, I realized I had missed the structure because I was looking for myself in it. I couldn't see the forest for the trees. It is beautiful. Just beautiful.

I thought perhaps Jan might need some of my poetry now to help her finish her journal, although it resolves itself already. Weak little words. I can't really say what I feel.

Jan on March 28, 1974

When Bea called me Tuesday night to tell me she had finished my journal, we agreed to meet the very next day. Why wait; let's get it over with.

Wednesday afternoon, she again entered my front door.
No I guess OK if it turns into a long Welsh let me I'm sorry if what if it turns into a long while oh that's OK sure She gave me her thirteen-page analysis of the events, her thinking and evaluation written during her Two Rivers R & R. "Weak little words," she wrote. "I can't really say what I feel."

Her sensitive analysis of my journal revealed honesty and insights and an evaluation of emotional trauma that revealed the intelligence and strength and maturity that I could count on, the stability I needed to know she had.

When Bea talked of my journal, rather than being visibly hurt or outraged by my plea of innocence and reasons for my actions, she took the rap for everything, the full responsibility, writing that "I do it for you. If you still want me to, I will. Warmer than ice, harder than rock, more durable than one lifetime. I'll never hurt you, Jan. Believe that. At least not intentionally. I never meant to hurt you, ever."

Jan on March 29, 1974

I have so much love to give and to share
that I stagger and tremble

under its weight as it grows
like enveloping tumors inside of me.
Will I ever be less vulnerable,
less susceptible or be immune
to these conditions that compel me—
guilelessly—into further complications.
For it is true, as diagnosed,
that I am prone to foster these involvements and
tenderly nurture the conditions
generating intimacy and love.

Is hurt my only remedy
and isolation of the prevention
with calculating reason used,
 a scalpel as the surgeon's tools.
I hope not! For then I choose
to live with this disease
and risk survival—incurable of this love
for people and for life.

Jan on March 30, 1974

At the end of our last meeting, Bea held out her hand at leaving me and I responded with mine—a parting gesture.

 It was now my time for my R&R. My family somehow disappeared somewhere and I read and reread each word she had written to me. I could think, write, revise, feel and evaluate. My insides were alive with the anticipation of xeroxing my revised journal that was finally true to me and to us. It now has the integrity it lacked.
 I did not see her Friday night at folk dancing. Saturday was empty, calm perhaps, but empty.
 I awoke in the dark of Sunday morning and my trembling self said she'd be in church and I'd hand her my envelope with this more honest evaluation of my life, this new me.
 I added a note on the envelope using her quote from her earlier letter, "Don't open this if you don't want to risk another landslide of emotion. Just return it unopened and I'll understand." In my letter, I

analyzed the concept I knew inside but she confirmed that the fear I had of her must have come from me and my past experiences.

<<<>>>

Bea, My fear of you was genuine; I was afraid. Yet you put it finally at rest when you said that fear must be from the bad memories of my childhood.

I started thinking and remembering and I realized why I couldn't accept your love.

It wasn't the love I couldn't take, but your irrational behavior when you were not alone with me. You were a different person during our afternoon talks. It wasn't the afternoons that scared me; it was the Friday nights.

You must understand that I couldn't love anyone who was not in control. I can't cope with uncertainties again after surviving erratic behavior from my youth, that I still experience when I visit my mother or when she visits me.

With this jarring of my fears, I relived the feeling of holding on—holding together tenuously by my fingertips all the strings and fiber in the fabric of my youth.

I cannot—I won't let this happen again to me.

I remember the shocking sound of shattered glass in the middle of the night when my mother shoved her fist through the windowpane and cold, shivering fear blew in through the space and through me. I remember my embarrassment of watching my father chase her as she ran half-naked out the front door. What would I have done if I'd been alone with her then? I remember tying her feet and hands to the bedposts so I could nap, exhausted after watching over her when my dad went to work—so she wouldn't hurt herself—or me. And the rainy night when the sheriff responded to a report about a woman with a dog pacing up and down a dead-end road. It was Mother and it was our dog. They picked up Mother, but I ran for hours that night screaming for my Lady.

I remember my father leaving me alone with her to join the Navy during World War II—leaving me when Mother was crazy, my living in a foster home, with her friends, with Grandma. He left me alone—with her—and I think then that I disliked her for making me suffer and I hated myself for being angry with someone I loved and who loved me but couldn't help being what she was. Talk about guilt!

No wonder I reject guilt now and avoid the compromises that create it. No wonder that the man I chose to marry is quiet and strong like a rock—insensitive perhaps and quietly aggressive too. I picked a person who's rational and evaluates every factor, who can be trusted to be in control.

No wonder I projected my forgotten fears when you drove recklessly, drank emotionally, stared at me, desperately held me in front of others and spilled out your feelings about us to Marge.

No wonder I hoped you would seek professional help because having you in control of yourself would release the thought that was going on in my head during these chaotic times, "If you get in control, perhaps I would let my natural child come out to play with your natural child."

But in my mind, you kept losing control—until last week. And when we talked on Sunday after your R&R and on Wednesday after you read my journal and after reading your beautiful writing during your R&R, I sensed power and stability in you to help us make decisions about our relationship that will benefit us both.

Jan

I was in turmoil. Life would be so much easier without this love. Why do I want to risk disaster? Just hold out for one more day—one day at a time. Who needs this?

But I was miserable and I savored every misery of it.

Bea on March 31, 1974

> I caught the bird of time
> and held it for a little while.
> Elusive bird, white with purity,
> red with the fire of life.
> I loved it, but it flew away.
> A free spirit, quicksilver, mercury.
> It left me a single white feather.

CHAPTER FIFTEEN

Jan on April 1, 1974

"I miss you, Bea," I said this morning when I answered her phone call that came immediately after my husband left for work. It was the truth and I never realized it so completely and honestly. I finally knew what she had been telling me was evident to her since November.

Not only did I miss her, but I loved her—really loved her.
What made me finally own up to my feelings was her stability finally revealed. She had picked herself up again after I had knocked her down. But this time, instead of lamenting and pleading, she showed me her strength, courage and intelligence.
With the dawn, I read without concentration and later sent my husband off to work. I watched the clock reach 7:55 a.m. and realized that I should get up to go to the bathroom. Maybe she would phone at 8.
What would I do if she didn't call?
I stepped out of the bathroom and the phone rang.
My heart stopped.
I picked it up—and it was Bea.
"Oh, Bea, I'm so glad it's you."

"I figured you'd be worried about me because I wasn't in church yesterday so I called to tell you I was having lunch in Milwaukee with Rachael."

"Oh. That's great!"

"Yeah." She paused. "How are you?"

What do I say? Do I want to start that landslide? Do I own up to my true feelings? Do I really want to get into this whole thing again? One day at a time. After hurting her again, will she tell me to go jump in the lake? How am I? I'm trembling, tired and finally honest with my feelings.

"I miss you, Bea!"

I had no sooner rushed Jenny out of the back door early to catch her school bus and leaped with each step charged to start my record player when Bea's green car flashed past my front window. I turned to look out the back window and saw Jenny plodding down the walk. I turned again toward the front window and saw Bea hopping over the curb and up my steps to ring the doorbell that sounded like an alarm to my electrified senses.

The dog barked as I opened the door and let Bea into the foyer.

My breathlessness ended, my tremors ignored, and I felt only the warmth of our reunion embrace and kiss, the profound tenderness and thrilling courage in our acceptance of our love.

For three hours, we loved and nurtured each other, embracing at tender levels of personal and emotional intimate intensity without naked sexually. We honestly, yet timidly, accepted and enjoyed the sensuality we shared. Unafraid, we were so hooked on these emotional and creative levels that carnal knowledge was not required. There would be time; there was no hurry.

Neither was possessed by the other; we shared equally in each other's love. Loving, loving, loving. We talked. We laughed. We forgot to eat or to drink. She didn't even smoke. We celebrated our love.

> A kiss that has to do
> with pure love, not only sex,
> but love that has to do
> with being
> a human being,

> a lover,
> a sweetheart,
> a friend, a sister/brother a wife/husband, a mother/daughter,
> a being being a being.

When it was time for her to go, the physical nourishment we chose to share was vodka on the rocks—to match the high spirits of ourselves. When she left, I felt completely beautiful and fully loved. And so happy. And honest—really honest because I allowed myself to finally be myself.

> I can't tell if it's the vodka
> or the essence of your presence
> in my memory which makes me
> heady as I open a goddamn can of Campbell's soup
> to nourish the physical me that hungers to be nurtured
> as completely as the emotional me.
> By the way—thanks.

That night I made love with Alex more fully and honestly than I have in months. I was complete. I was all-human. I was totally loved, totally loving and euphorically happy.

> I have so much love to give and to share
> that I stagger and shudder under its weight
> as it grows like enveloping tumors inside of me.
> Will I ever be less vulnerable,
> less susceptible or immune
> to these conditions that compel me,
> guilelessly, into further complications.
> For it is true, as diagnosed, I am prone
> to foster these involvements and tenderly nurture
> the conditions generating intimacy and love.
> Is hurt my only remedy and isolation the prevention
> with calculating reason used, a scalpel as the surgeon's tools.
> I hope not! For then I choose to live with this disease
> and risk survival—
> incurable of this love for people and for life.

Jan on April 2, 1974

Still euphoric, I woke from a deep sleep in the soul of my being. I could hardly move from the physical exhaustion of being loved intensely and yet tenderly. I felt I'd cracked my ribs. My lame, weary arms were powerless, but the part of me that hurt the most was my face—from smiling so broadly and joyfully.

> You give me gladness as a gift—
> A most precious offering most heartily received,
> most gratefully acknowledged,
> most joyously celebrated gladness,
> sublime, supreme, superb
> gladness inside.
>
> It only hurts when I laugh
> Not my new shirt and I'm laughing all the time
> and I hurt so good.

I groaned each time I moved and then laughed about how good it felt. I thought of Bea each time I moved and each time I stayed still.

I had an hour's tennis lesson at 4 p.m. and I couldn't serve. I couldn't return the ball. I told the pro I'd had a sore back from Friday's doubles game with Alex and I'd "taken a back treatment that left me lame," I said with a telling smile that hinted at being loved to numbness.

Jan on April 3, 1974

One VW camper van and one sedan parked next to each other right before dusk on the outer edge of the UW's farthest, most unused parking lot, halfway between Lakeshore Bay and North Grove. The sedan's bumper sticker said, "Sailors have more fun." The other said, "Another Mother for Peace."

It was an absurd meeting for the two women in their early forties sitting together in one car—and dangerous too—just as this narration is dangerous. Yet the flaunting of convention and the intrigue of meeting and the anticipation of being found together—

two mature women talking and holding and loving each other tenderly while parked either in remote places or inconspicuous corners—added a delectable spice to this heady diet of tasting love's first hors d'oeuvres.

Our VW camper bus took on a new life dashing smartly forward down back roads and parkways to join her. The "I'm Hooked on a Feeling" song with its primitive "Oga chucka, oga chucka" beat chanted through my head. My whole compulsive self was centered on being with her. Our reckless meetings that were so desperately needed empowered me since I realized my potential for love.

Because of the part-time element of my hospital job, I had the time options to arrange my life to fit into my schedule yet still maintain my family responsibility and my job requirements.

Bea and I knew we had to carry on this insatiable love affair while driving children to school and meeting every deadline, supper time, marriage and time functions. We wanted our marriage and families to survive with us. We did not want to reject these commitments and these values. We wanted to rearrange our former selves so that we would be able to fill the other needs we shared; our personal and internal priorities were fulfilled while our external responsibilities were met.

I phoned her to say that I had to see her. If I didn't see her before the church's annual dinner tomorrow, I'd not be able to carry out our masquerade.

Marge had told us to "divorce each other," to break off our friendship until cooler heads could prevail. The dinner would be a test of our coolness under scrutiny. Bea said she thought she'd sit with Susan and Ken Majors on the opposite side of the room. Space would help. We would manage to hide our true feelings.

"Don't throw bouquets at me…" I sang. "People will say we're in love."

We held each other and I started rocking my beautiful friend—with ultimate tenderness in our togetherness.

I am Mother Earth. Mother Earth is M.E.

Jan on April 5, 1974

I had to celebrate. I cherished her so much. Yet I felt that seeing her at folk dancing would set off a charge in me that I couldn't control in front of the others.

When I phoned asking her to meet me, she responded at a moment's notice. We'd met for coffee at the pancake house once before in November. Then she trembled before me. Now it was my turn. But this time, I was the fortunate one because, unlike before, our love was mutual.

We took an impulsive ride into Petrifying Springs and actually parked in a spot off the road. "I can comfort a friend in need. Her dog just died," was my rehearsed line if we were questioned by roving park police.

We talked and laughed. Our tenderness made us feel innocent because of our self-imposed touching limits. "There is no hurry to test the hardness of this new power that we've discovered." I wrote that line a month earlier. Our complete acceptance of each other continued to inspire spontaneous poems, sentences and paragraphs of deepest feelings of understanding and compassion, even as we realized how roughly we could be punished if we were discovered.

That night I watched her folk dancing. I watched her sitting at the party afterward. I watched her smiling. My mind was conversing with hers without exchanging words. Words were meaningless; our thoughts connected us.

I was stunned by her humor, her openness, her strength and control and her warmth, especially when she initiated a conversation and teased Pete about his homemade wine. If that were me, I probably would have kicked him in the groin for taking advantage of my vulnerability.

Then I led her by the hand to the second floor to show her how cleverly the girls had decorated their rooms and we were alone. Standing apart in case someone would find us, I said, "When you stared at me from across that room full of folk dancers, you looked at me and you etched your image forever into my memory—the portrait of the most beautiful human being I know." We moved closer. She touched my shoulder and I crumbled inside for an instant before newcomers entering our reality startled us.

It was ironic that Marge joined us. Did she think I needed rescuing again?

Bea had carried her guitar with her, quickly sat on one of the beds and started to sing "Words," the song she'd written for me, the song that repeats itself endlessly in my mind.

Earlier, I told Bea the other line that I was rehearsing. If Marge asks me what's up with Bea and me, I'll announce boldly, "I'm celebrating the most beautiful love affair that anyone has experienced."

Marge hadn't heard the song and when it was finished, we followed her down the narrow stairs to step out the door that opened into the party. I was last in line behind Bea. Marge stopped at the bottom stair with Bea following and I moved forward. When our two bodies touched, the energy current seemed to create an aura around the two of us, separating us from everyone else in the room. Bea whispered quietly over her shoulder, "We keep this up and you may have to use that speech you've rehearsed for Marge."

Jan on April 7, 1974

Saturday—a whole day yesterday without seeing or talking with her— and yet we were together as we anticipated our next meeting and remembered those that had passed.

I'm so happy sitting in my sensuous, floor-length, red jersey tube dress while sipping a martini in my home, all alone with my memories. My thoughts bring tears to my eyes and joy to my heart as the phonograph plays Cat Stevens' sad songs of unrequited love.

Remembering butterflies in symbolic flight and her gaze turning soft from tenderness rather than tears, I'm still filled with pulses beating as I feel her body, clothed and next to mine, warm and responsive to my touch and mine to hers.

"Tell Rachael that we're both OK and to have fun in San Francisco," I said to Rachael's daughter when I phoned to leave a message from the two of us, and Rachael's daughter declared, "She will!"

And as I end these poetic thoughts before I go to bed, Helen Reddy's record falls from my LP stack and she sang, "You bring the music out in me...Hey, hey, I'm a bit OK. Thanks...Hey, what, think I'm such a hotshot? Why not when you look at what I've got...So we've lived together through another whole day...." And I've swapped emptiness for fulfillment. I'll not openly flaunt convention or encourage the envy of others. What we have is too precious. I won't risk losing it again. I'm happy.

CHAPTER SIXTEEN

Jan on April 9, 1974

Sundays at our Unitarian church without a minister and without Alex off to find one can be an emotional environment filled with dear friends or challenging opponents participating in worshipful sharing or confrontations with exchanges of views. Yet this Sunday generated a perfect tone.

Somehow among announcements to sign the "Save the Bears" petition and watching a presentation on prison reform, my mood changed when the congregation was asked for their expressions of joy and concern. My face turned to find Bea; our two smiles shouted joy without a sound across the sanctuary.

Later we spoke at an awkward distance with a church pew between us. What we said were innocuous words about tennis and sore muscles and "playing with me" and our eyes sparkled with the double meanings.

She gave me a crystal with her poem "... a lovely multi-sided crystal, pure and translucent, warmer than ice, harder than rock, more durable than one lifetime." I took it home to set it with an empty shell she'd given me earlier.

During the quiet afternoon, I couldn't forget the deep russet brown eyes that looked at me in love, but then, I didn't want to forget them—ever.

Mother Earth's eyes enfold me
in their natural, nurturing beauty.
And I, as Nature's own,
creep along the stamen
to sample the sweet goodness
of the lush flower to unearth the secrets
of its great power.

I spent yesterday reliving these days and decided to recreate and retain the beautiful hours and sentiments that we've shared. I typed all this day, but I completed only April 1st and 2nd. I'm not making a mistake by journaling, but I must be careful that no one finds it. I want to remember and savor every moment forever. I'll do anything to be with Bea and I'll write everything in prose or in poetry. I can't believe I'm in the throes of an affair with Bea, with a woman, recklessly, wildly abandoning all thought over what can happen to her, and to me writing down everything and then hiding it when I finish until I can share it with her.

I must keep this one a secret, unlike my original journal that I shared with Bea first, then Marge and Rachael. I'm saving one copy for my daughter to have when she is old enough to appreciate its inspired nuances.

Of course, Bea devoured it, reading it several times. And Rachael mailed me a letter dated April 7.

Dear Jan

I'm on the plane to San Francisco and I took your journal along to read. Thank you—for the warm creeping joy I'm feeling before I've even had my special treat of a Bloody Mary in the morning at high altitude, for sharing with me your enormously beautiful searching, yearning rich self, for the thrill of being included as important in that search. Your work, as a part of you, has strength and grace and universality and the tremendous power of a woman's infinite capacity for love. I feel rich—sensually and emotionally and fortunate in knowing you and in walking the same unexplored tentative yet sure trails. Thank you most of all for being you.

With love and with respect (Love I'm generous with, respect beyond that of respect for humanness, I give with great discrimination.)

Rachael

I called Bea and said, "Hello."

The effervescent voice from the other end of the line said, "What a beautiful poem 'Hello' is. My poem to you is, 'Were I a real witch, I'd make Monday disappear entirely—a useless day except when I spend it smiling.'"

We are to meet this afternoon.

I raced through my chores at home and then at work, anxiously waiting for 11:30 a.m. when we had our appointment to meet again. I was working, but my mind was writing poetry filled with intimacy and inspiration and the power of thought based on the force of love.

My power was expansive and explosive, especially at work when an important person I couldn't ignore came into my office to talk with me right when I was ready to leave. I could see the timepiece tick the seconds that were running out for me to get home before she arrived.

Minutes are momentous. Assorted persons keep coming and going and I didn't want to waste the precious minutes between the going of one and the coming of the other.

11:05

11:08

I was listening and responding to my office visitor, but I was not there. Mentally I was leaping into my car to drive the few blocks home.

11:11

I was free to be me— Alexa set timer for 2:30

At 11:40, we were alone together again in my studio office upstairs in my home. My son came and went and we were alone together again— she wore her body blouse surrounding her torso under her black slacks—and we, with an adolescent caution of

physical intimacy, had the warmest and woolliest loving afternoon. The floor was a roomy place to make love, roomy for even the inexperienced teenage techniques we used—groping to find satisfaction. Much of our gratification, corny though it seems, came from expressing poetic thoughts. Much was spent in coping with the artificial restraints we placed on our being together—body shirts, shoes, boots, clothing that were in our way because we anticipated being caught together. We were ready and poised to reassemble ourselves back to clothed respectability, absurd though the scramble could be.

No man would put up with these restraints. He'd move and extend and thrust home—clothes or no. Yet we, perhaps symbolically, refused to love at that level. Perhaps, psychologically, we jeopardized the physical gratification that lovers set as standards for their love.

The floor was a roomy place, but hard and rough too and my poor elbows were skinned raw with scrapes from the harsh, woven surface of the rug, scuff marks that I carried for weeks of remembering.

It was wild. It was tender. It was joyous, intense—and sad. She had not really permitted herself the freedom to love as I granted myself.

She said to me words I can call on to reinforce my acceptance of us together, words that give perspective to our urgent frenzy. In our creative exchanges of intimacies, she said that one needs a single point of reference to fix a vision. "When the intensity of our feelings has lessened, we'll be such great friends. Such a friendship—like the Gemini twins in the sky."

While eating out for supper with the family, I performed the routine, but my body seemed like a vague shadow and my mind looked inside itself, in retrospection.

When we returned home, the phone was ringing. I answered it and heard her broken-spirited voice talking from the tiny, crowded cubicle that she uses for privacy.

She had confronted Jake about their relationship saying, "I have a feeling that I've been separated or divorced for a long time and no one told me about it." In her need for both kinds of love to reassure herself of her bisexuality, she made him realize what their marriage was like by putting those words in his thoughts—words that were too clever for him to appreciate.

She wrote a script for him. It was an easy way out and he accepted it as a chance to reject her and her creative, complex intensity.

Did I force her to make this move?

In many ways, the sadness in her manner this afternoon, the directness and determination that she set in her loving of me, was a prelude to the directness and determination in confronting her husband.

She had loved me and I had loved her—emotionally.

She wanted her husband to love her as she loved him—physically.

Perhaps more vital, she also wanted to have the same reassurance gained from my relationship with my husband. She then could release the years of doubts and frustrations in the shadows of her mind. A premonition of sadness haunted this sharing of honest responses. I felt her need for reassurance in accepting this relationship and I needed reassurance too because I revealed to her my last piece of deception when I told her that I'd Xeroxed all of her letters that she wanted returned and destroyed. I had given her the originals and never told her that I had made copies.

"They're my letters too," I said. "And I did not want to lose them."

Instead of anger or resentment for my deception, she responded with love and understanding by saying she was complimented at having her letters preserved by me.

Most people think of simplistic either/or definitions and limitations. For them, thoughts and emotions are either rational or genital polarities, of the head or of the groin. Few have the emotional perception and security to grasp both extremes, plus all the esoteric subtleties in between. I used to think that I was the

"Suzanne" in the Leonard Cohen/Judy Collins song. Now I know it's Bea who is Suzanne—or maybe both of us are to each other.

> "… And you want to travel with her,
> And you want to travel blind,
> And you think maybe you'll trust her,
> For you've touched her perfect body
> With your mind."

Jan on April 11, 1974

When the phone rang yesterday at 8 a.m., Bea spoke in stronger tones as if the open-heart surgery performed in pain and fear was over now. The patient was going to be healthier and stronger. She said this confrontation with her husband was related to her definition of faith: "You step on the pad to open the electric door in the supermarket and you keep on walking through because you know it'll open. It didn't work and I broke my nose."

Today our first consciousness-raising group topic in the church's Hearth Room was appropriately scheduled with a touch of predetermination giving Bea a chance to evaluate her home situation.

Months earlier, Marge invited me to join the church's first women's rap group, but I had turned it down because I was too busy. When I was free to join the group, Marge turned me down because the women had bonded with honest and intimate details of their lives and any newcomer would be an intruder. OK. But this was the first time I'd ever been turned away from one of our groups and it bothered me until now when I was to be in this second group led by Betty McGregor. Now I was with my Bea, so it was meant to be.

We were given a list of fifteen subjects with several questions under each category that gave us a chance to set the group's discussion priorities and each week, we'll know the next topic and have that time to think and remember our experiences. The questions we started talking about were: 1) How was womanhood presented to you as a child? 2) What expectations were you supposed to fulfill? 3) What do you think of womanhood now?

When Bea talked in the group, her humor showed genius with traces of what TA would call "gallows laughter." I was intensely proud of her and happy for her to have this circle of women who had childhood problems related more closely to hers than to mine; that is; no one else but me was raised by a schizophrenic mother. The sessions reinforced our shared malaise of our women's experience and absurd husband/family situations where we live in homes in which our individual lives have no meaning other than to serve.

For example, Joanne spoke of growing up with four brothers and, like her mother, she was supposed to help take care of all the males in her family. "But I learned a lot from the boys, rode motorcycles, skied and had lots of fun with guys as I grew older. Because I went to bars after work, where I met my husband, I became more independent, but I didn't meet my mother's expectations and there's bickering and hostility between us even today.

"Of course, suing my boss for sexual harassment isn't easy," she added. "And my husband doesn't seem to support me. He probably thinks I'll lose. It seems to embarrass my five teenage kids, too. We'll see what happens when I'm done with all this."

Marie's father was an Army colonel and her mother was an Army-dependent housewife. "My father, of course, used strict discipline over my mother and me, an only child. I guess that's why I'm so casual about my kids and look how much they misbehave," she said as she shrugged her shoulders. "I loved my father and I inherited his intelligence, that I know, but I don't know what to do with it. At this time, I see myself more like my mother, but that's because our boys are young. Just wait until they get older and I can begin a career that I've put on hold when I married."

After having lunch with Bea, I went to my Lakeshore Med's office.

The desks for four employees that come and go at odd hours barely leave room to walk about. Two small basement windows, high and at ground level, cast a dim northern light from a courtyard walled in by the original brick hospital built a century ago. The office door is half a window and our office ceiling lights and desk lamps illuminate the poorly lit corridor and attract the eyes of passers-by who peer at us.

"Stan and Mike must have finished early again today," Randy said, turning his swivel chair in my direction. He leaned back, put his hands behind his head, took a deep breath and stretched.

I turned my chair away from my typewriter. "Mike must be out on his second shift rounds and I'm finished writing the newsletter.

I've been thinking a lot about what we've been talking about and if it's OK with you, I thought, maybe I'd show you this poem I wrote last month, if you have time to read it?" I unfolded a single sheet of bond paper, its creases pressed in my wallet and I handed it to him.

"It's short," he said. "Only five stanzas. Sure. I'll read it now." I watched him read it and he looked up and said, "It flows nicely. I like the collage metaphor you use." He read aloud.

> "I want to dissolve the outer film,
> strip away the old veneers
> of double standards and injustice,
> pettiness and hurt that hinder me."

I looked up and out the basement window, attracted by the slippered feet of patients that appeared in the courtyard, the occasional sunny day, and a late afternoon volleyball outing for psych unit patients. The ball often hit sedated patients before they reacted quickly enough to return the volleyball.

But Randy's quiet voice is what I hear.

> "If I survive the revelations
> of what is under all,
> I will emerge clean and strong,
> free to be honest with myself,
> to know truly what I am."

He raised his eyes from the paper. "It's hard to believe. Surely you know who you are."

"Does anyone truly know, for certain?"

His raised eyebrows added temporary wrinkles to his brow. He pulled on his tie as he shifted in his chair. "Humm." Again he read.

> "Happily expecting
> to find the beauty that's within,
> yet preparing for a shock,
> I await the discovery of who I really am."

Suddenly, the volleyball hit the black mesh grid over our window. A vague but grinning face peered in and his flaccid hand fluttered an apologetic wave for the interruption. Across the courtyard, an aide blew her whistle and the muted game of overmedicated puppets continued.

"I hardly think you'd shock anyone," he said. "You have things under control, your family, your life." He paused. "How strange that you feel this ambivalence."

"You mean that people my age should know who they are and that only handsome young philosophers like yourself are searching?"

"Well, I'm confused too. Where will my career take me? Will I find happiness if I get married?" He leaned closer. "I was especially confused when I was away at school. So many guys were gay." He looked away and returned to the poem.

"But, you're such a lady's man and in such demand. You can have any woman you want."

"Yes," he moved back and smiled furtively, "And I have to have a woman five or six times a week to prove it." He watched for my reaction to his insinuating wanton promiscuity.

"Well, your reputation is true then," I smiled back without revealing my appreciation for his freedom to josh about his maleness and yet, if so, my weighing a wary concern for the women he may be using. "What a busy young man you are."

"And a tired one, too."

"It sounds like a struggle—to keep up that pace. I'm sure you don't have time to write any poetry."

"Not really, not at all. How do you find the time?"

"Oh, that comes out of me naturally now," I said as we waved to a colleague walking past the light of our office door window shining into the dark hall.

Jan on April 13, 1974

Alex and I took Pete Kramer and his wife Josie with us to see Shakespeare's contemporary Christopher Marlowe's *The Tragicall Historie of Dr. Faustus*. We had tickets, or we probably wouldn't have gone, but my perception and appreciation for the universal truths in this play affirmed my openness to living my life beyond others' standards. I identified with this spectacularly produced spectrum of feelings and philosophies. The hero, the highly successful Faust who was dissatisfied with his life, made a pact with the Devil to exchange his soul for unlimited knowledge and worldly pleasures, including Helen of Troy, the most beautiful of women.

When Helen appeared before Faustus in a shimmering light, I knew the true meaning of the famous quote about Helen and the Trojan War, "Is this the face that launched a thousand ships," and I could feel his, as is my own, overwhelming love.

Jan on April 14, 1974

I woke early in anticipation—but not for Easter. I was so completely exhausted that I couldn't plan or prepare for holiday rites and family dinners. They'd have to take care of me or have nothing. My family enjoyed it more than anything because the four of us planned to spend a gentle day.

I woke in anticipation of the chance to see her again, even if it was only in a crowd at church. Actually, it's fun being in a group and communicating with her in our own way.

But it can be dangerous.

We attended the pancake brunch after the church service and I sat across from Bea who was expounding on some thesis or other to her daughter sitting at her side. My family settled in with friends elsewhere in the room. While I was concentrating on what Bea had to say, I slipped away from conscious thought and stared into those deep Mother Earth eyes. The intensity registered and while she continued her words while looking at me, she too lost her thoughts, halted, hesitated and in the moment's pause, forgot completely what she was saying and stared intensely back at me. It may have seemed blank to many, but to me, it was the most potent laser beam of feeling that has ever been exchanged between human beings. When we recovered and came back to reality, we laughed quietly together at this—what else could we do? Good thing not too many noticed—or maybe no one noticed at all.

When we parted, she said, "Listen, you know what kind of privacy I have at home. We'll have to be like Bacall and Bogart and say, "If you want me, just whistle—" And the expression was never more relevant. I whistled and she came. We met for lunch at our spot, but we forgot to eat. She has a knack for hinting at potential interludes or timing her messages so that when we part, ideas linger until we meet again. Or she uses touch to project more meaningful encounters to come. My body shivers. I get dizzy when I see her. But more so, the sensation increases during the time we're apart. The progression of our love is advancing to more mature encounters.

Jan on April 18, 1974

Tuesday was the only blank day on my calendar. But my mind and my body are not blank from remembering yesterday and anticipating two complete days together.

(The Faustus play was the last memory that I typed in documenting our acceptance of love, loyalty, friendship, sensual, bi-sexual, love-centered, life-expanding, poetic, creative living. Because I had crowded every possible moment of time that we could be together, I could not write every day but recreated only to this last entry. It was fortunate that I fell behind because the closing sentence of our April 14 encounter says it all: "The progression of our love is growing and advancing to more mature encounters." It's been months, a year or more before I'd return to complete journaling my "Thank You for April," and I added continuing events months later, again in chronological order.).

CHAPTER SEVENTEEN

Jan on April 17 and 18, 1974

I freed myself from home and work by signing up for UW's respectable Weekend College event, skipping our rap group discussions on our early family backgrounds. Bea and I were more motivated by what would develop during our two days together.

Bea was tense when I arrived at her home to take her to our workshops. It was rare when her many teens were gone. How long would they stay away? Our being together has always been tenuous, but with so many of their friends coming in and out, we'd be discovered together and that would be a disaster.
She gave me a gift of Jovan grass oil perfume: "For my beloved Mother Earth. All my love." I dabbed it on and we enjoyed our earthy senses together before we left for our workshops.
Yes, we went to our Wednesday classes and listened to lectures on Ellis Albert's stress and tension of poor inter-personal relations, Tolstoy's *Death of Ivan Ilyich* and the five stages of grief, a workshop on "The Permissive Society," Albert Ellis' *Guide to Rational Living* and Abraham Maslow's *Toward a Psychology of Being* listing the principles of the self-actualizing person.
We sat in swiveling lecture hall seats, our knees and shoes touching, our hands brushing against each other when we were not

taking notes. The intellectual stimulus was affirming what we felt each of us to be.

The self-actualizing person has a
- superior perception of reality,
- increased acceptance of self, of others and of nature,
- increased spontaneity,
- increase in problem centering,
- increased detachment and desire for privacy,
- increased autonomy and resistance to enculturation,
- greater freshness of appreciation and richness of emotional reaction,
- higher frequency of "peak experiences",
- increased identification with the (whole) human species,
- improved interpersonal relationships,
- more democratic character structure,
- increased creativity,
- and certain changes in the value system.

It's a peak experience each time we're together. How rare is that?

While driving to pick her up for our next day together, I was memorizing the dialogue from Faustus that I wanted to recite to her. It was strange driving the Volkwagan camping van, shifting gears through busy streets and tooling past parks while rhapsodizing about Helen of Troy.

Yes, we skipped classes on the second day but gained an A+ in our continuing education which had nothing to do with the university. We were learning to love each other physically as we have emotionally. We'd made love to each other within the bounds we'd set up for ourselves—except for the shoes we took off, sometimes. Even with our initial, delicate, intense desires, Bea, especially, was not giving herself permission to be free.

She packed a picnic lunch with a bottle of wine and directed me out of town to a shady spot south along the lakeshore. We talked in detail about the lectures from the previous day. Her intelligence, her recall of what was said and what she had studied in her reading filled me with awe and respect. We walked out on the sand to pick wild dry weeds bouquets for each of us. We looked for shells, for fossils in the rocks and we teetered across the concrete rubble mounds that protected the shore from erosion.

I was weak with fatigue from the fervor, from the lack of sleep because of my early waking in anticipation, from the bone-weary schedule of my many duties and activities. I slid open the camper's side door to sit in the van's upright back seat, and she followed me in. I collapsed my head on her shoulder to rest from the intense forbidden emotional commitment we were undertaking.

And I'd promised myself to speak of Faustus and Helen of Troy. "Bea, I hope I can remember this correctly. At the play the other night, I watched Faustus sell his soul to the devil to fill his desire to gain knowledge of all things. Like a glutton, Faustus asked Mephistopheles to fulfill the longing of his heart's desire by having as his lover the divine Helen of Troy. While watching the play, I lost myself by understanding exactly what he experienced."

I touched Bea's shoulder with my hand and spoke softly in her ear, "The most beautiful woman entered the scene dressed in a sheer white gown. She said nothing. She hardly moved, but she glowed with sensuality. Faust looked at her—and suddenly, I knew the meaning of one of the most hokey phrases. 'Is this the face that launched a thousand ships? Sweet Helen, make me immortal with a kiss.'"

Rising to my knees to seem taller and more Faustian, I took Bea's face in my hands to kiss her most gentle lips.

"Sweet Helen, make me immortal with a kiss. Her lips," I quoted, "suck forth my soul—see where it flies!" And I kissed her again as Faustus had done to Helen. "Come, Helen, come, give me my soul again." And my own soul was one united with hers in our love as no one else has loved. "Here will I dwell, for heaven is in these lips."

Dare I be bolder? And inhaling a terrified yet excited breath as if I were about to leap off a cliff into the water below, I finally had the audacity to slowly adjust my arm to slip down around her shoulders to her back and under her arm. My body pressed closer, and my hand reached even further around her slimness as I drew her to me and touched her body shirt gently to caress her breast. I felt her inhale for air, for oxygen, for the courage to step beyond and into the next level of love.

I hesitated when she moved, hardly breathing, to stare out her window. I took her silence as permission to embrace her from behind her back with each hand holding her breasts as I pressed the front of my body into her and tongued the nape of her neck and the crevices in her shoulders.

The taboos of a hostile society to what we were doing made our immature advances headier and charged. The restraints of her buttons and bodysuit, snapped between her legs, giving her control over how far we would go. Also, our internalized fears of what would happen next and how we would cope made each tiny touch a turning point toward "the love that dare not speak its name."

After accepting my touch, she turned to look at me with soft yet focused determination as she slowly started unbuttoning my shirt to touch the surface of my bra and cautiously explore the warmth of my chest. With Lake Michigan's waves gently lapping against the shore in front of us, we were learning to receive and give sensual love from another woman with unhurried, intense and guileless intimacy. It was our hungry lips savoring the taste, gasping for breath, wanting more, yet our clothed bodies matched each other's contours in the fire of friction that joined us together.

"I have never experienced this complete love for another human being. It is what I have been searching for, this love that totally envelops me with joy."

Kissing and talking quietly, we were completely honest, open, and deep, like unborn twins in utero, yet more like adult children with shared women's experiences. Yet also adolescents again—Romeo and Juliet were hiding together in their secret love. Bea and I were alive together, thriving together on the glorious nourishment of our hungry selves; beings transformed into one being; transported into a higher existence.

Was it because our love was forbidden that made it so completely intoxicating, so desirable, compelling, intense and overwhelming? Forbidden, yes, forbidden even beyond having an extra-marital heterosexual affair. But this love of a woman is so natural and basic to women who must fulfill their lives, needs that have been hidden from history and society, condemned and defamed because we need no man and because it feels so good.

Yes, the heady emotion of love—and the power of it coming from the subjects of that love—two courageous women who found the soul mates each had been seeking: a passionate lover, a trusted sister, a nurturing mother, a true friend.

"I want to shout out our love from the rooftops," I again declared, firmly but quietly.

"You'll get us in enough trouble with that writing of yours," Bea warned.

Together in this space, so close, encircling each other, Bea's brown eyes merging into my blues, we saw in each other's reflection the spirit of our own souls.

CHAPTER EIGHTEEN

Jan on April 18, 1974

Another Door County weekend at our Woodridge land, enjoying our husbands-and-wives guests who slept at a nearby motel. I feed them at-home-made stews, now defrosted and simmering on a two-burner Coleman stove under a screened-in tent, or brats and burgers grilled on the Weber, beer, other beverages and martinis, shopping, touring favorite sites, swimming and bathing in nearby Buckaroo Lake, enjoying the clear starry nights and fresh spring storms and the clean air following the rain with a rainbow spanning the horizon.

And when I wasn't involved in adult conversations, my mind was thinking of my lonesome lover back home. I had no need for electric power, showers and flush toilets, nor portable radio music because my internal dialogue with its own songs filled my inner self.

Bea on April 18, 1974

On a school bus chaperoning a field trip to the Museum of Science and Industry with my daughter's class, I climb back into the attic of my mind where all my treasures are and run tape recordings of the last few days. Phrases race through my mind for my Critical Parent to use to beat me: enculturation, crushes, latent lesbian, mutual masturbation.

> What do you want to do?
> Drift into total homosexuality?"
> You must leave, Jan.
> What are we doing?

Oh, God! Oh, God! Let me know when I stop feeling guilty. Let ME know. I was never able to do anything about it. I couldn't stop myself.

Critical Parent, leave me alone! I LOVE and am LOVED. That is more important to me than phrases, platitudes, and adopted values handed to me by previous madmen. Help me, LOVE. Help me, my beloved, to conquer this Parent, to conquer all.

Jan on April 20, 1974

Dear Rachael,

For once, I'm at a loss for words. Your overwhelming response to my poems left me breathless and gave me a feeling of being profoundly worthy, especially when they come from my friendly, newly certified Transactional Analyst Psychologist.

Your words planted a seed for a book that I'd share with everyone on, and I quote you, "…the tremendous power of a woman's infinite capacity for love." I've said your words over and over again and that's the secret of my strength.

And we all have the potential for the same if we'd risk it.

I went to a Weekend College last Friday and Saturday and discovered I've passed with an A++ on all of Maslow's tests for being a "self-actualizing person" who, with more friends like you, can be and is euphoric again in the truest, widest sense of the feeling.

Love,
Jan

Jan on April 25, 1974

I'm drawn to my little study at the top of the stairs, my secret soul place where I reveal my new self to me and to Bea, writing, creating, and revising what I wrote the night before sitting in a stupor of love and wine.

But when the others living in my huge house have gone to bed and I'm alone downstairs in my favorite chair with my wild emotions, my liberated thoughts, my remembering the turbulence of my newfound love, I find a pencil and any scrap of paper to capture my thoughts to keep forever—at least until the next day when I try to decipher the scrawl.

My first thoughts this morning are that I'll be seeing Bea soon. My second thoughts are to find where I tucked last night's notes. I can't have anyone find what I've written. When I remembered where the words were, I captured them in my pocket. My next thought is, what do I make Matt for breakfast to give him the high carbohydrates that he needs for his long-distance running obsession?

My relationship life has changed from Alex in high school and college, teenage love with slightly older Karen, marriage to Alex for almost 25 years and raising Matt and preteen sister Jenny, then a deep, unrequited crush with our friend Marge that stopped my boredom and loneliness, now to electrifying excitement and emotional gratification. I have found my soul sister. She loves me and I love her and we're both crazy and obsessed with each other.

As I finish my other life's duties for husband, son and daughter and, as they leave, my focus gets clearer and my anticipation pumps energy toward myself and my Bea, who will join me as soon as she completes her other-life duties.

The back doors close, the car starts, my husband drives away, my children leave for school, and I approach my hidden writing. My handwriting is illegible as I read those heady words; soon the writing takes more form, the words get larger and the penciled phrases evolve from hapless meanderings. And I laugh and wonder why the thoughts expressed are so good, so clear, so universal, joyful, yet sad about the lost time before this moment.

After checking the downstairs rooms to see that everything is respectable and that the kitchen stove is turned off, I'm a racer, a hurdler turning the corner, grabbing the banister and bounding up my multicolored carpet-sample treads that I installed on my stairs. "I built a stairway to Paradise, with a new step every day!" sings through my brain—each stair colored in sequence by carpet sample pieces leading from dark hues to light golden shades at the top.

Taking a sharp hairpin turn into my studio, I slide into my typing nook to translate my feelings, deciphering last night's words that fall into place.

Bea will be here soon.

Then I make myself fresh and clean in a slow, hot, sensuous shower to cool me down. I have to be careful not to fall as I move quickly again when I realize that the time is coming for her to join me. I don't want anything negative to happen when my life is so fine as I juggle and balance all that is required of me, including another important detail, my writing career with two part-time positions, one in hospital communications and the other as a newspaper feature writer.

Jeans and a shirt with buttons on the front, that's what I'll wear. And brushing my short hair into place, I'm ready to resume my writing.

She's coming. I know. I can feel it. And I stand up to peer out my studio window to see her bounding up the long, narrow walk toward my back door. She is so slim. Cold. She looks cold. And frail. But resolute. Her long dark hair framing her face accents the determination she transmits with her eyes. Her black boots with heels clicking on the concrete alert me to her sense of purpose as she disappears under my porch roof and into my house. Coming into the door and up the five steps, she opens the kitchen door and calls out my name.

I'm nailed to the spot at the same time that my inner self leaps to get to her. We have to be careful of the kitchen windows because my neighbor often looks out the window at her sink and she may see Bea in the house.

"I'm up in the studio," and Bea bounded up to unite with me in my arms at the top of the stairs, two new lovers blissfully embracing.

We caught each other at the top of the stairs and after standing, embracing, I started to kneel with her following me. I lay my lover on my rainbow patchwork rug like a queen would lay her treasured gift on an altar cloth. As we progressed within our limits, if we rolled together too vigorously, we could tumble together down the stairs.

Frustrated with her ever-present, self-containing bodysuit, I took the initiative to unsnap her shirt, and finally, I was able to reach and touch the edge of her pubic line, planning cautiously to give her greater satisfaction than ever before. The intense feeling of this new intimacy combined with the danger of having anyone walk into the house and up the stairs for forgotten school books or misplaced memos gave me the boldness to act further, to touch her bareness, her warmth, and for the first time, she surrendered to me.

She was no passive captive. Simultaneously I sensed her hands and fingers on me and I stroked her as I stroked myself to give me pleasure as I listened to her response to guide me. It was not without other hazards, as clothes could only be parted up or down from her waist. Nor was it without her hands touching, reaching for any part of me she could touch through my clothes as I hovered above her. I would kiss her warm bareness around her belly, tease her navel but not to her distraction, and breathe in her musky, womanly fragrance.

I wrapped my legs around one of hers, my aroused pubic mons on her knee. Years of tennis gave me strength, yet I grew stronger, one arm holding me up with that hand under her, my fingers cupped to press her against me. Her body arched to meet mine. My other hand gently entered her essence, sensitively, so sensitively that she continued to trust my learning fingers and thrust herself upon them. My thumb gently massaged her clitoris as my fingers delicately delved into her velvety, moist sanctuary. After stroking and moving in rhythm, our senses reached the peak of breathless tension, my entire body shared her climax and we two became one woman coming together.

Not to calculate for better or for worse
but just (How grand a just!) to be.

Bea on April 26, 1974

Jan called me on a noontime work errand from a phone booth at Larry's Liquor Store corner. I think she was thinking more about what she was to say than about where she said it because I could hardly hear her and she could hardly hear me. I couldn't speak loudly, even from my little cubbyhole space next to the washer and dryer. Someone here could hear me, and she was surrounded by grinding concrete mixers and bulldozers repairing the intersection.

"I found the first payphone I could to call you. I can't stop thinking about you. I'm obsessed with you. My body aches for you."

"My body too." And with her most sensual voice kissing my ear, she moaned, "I can still feel you. This is the first time I've had such a climax. You gave me a heady ride through the stratosphere, dear."

"Can you talk louder? I can't hear you and I don't want to miss a word."

"I can't hear you well either, but I can't talk any louder. Jake's here. He and Josh are going off to see about Josh's joining the Army." But she repeated her first statement a bit louder, but not much. I wanted her to shout from her rooftop so I could hear her in Lakeshore Bay.

"I hope I didn't hurt you!"

"No. No. Nothing like that."

"Oh, that's good. That's the last thing I would want to do. And I can feel you too. I'll never forget that feeling. And I hope you'll let me do that again soon."

" But I hear loud bells ringing in my ears."

"Me too. That's only the bulldozer backing up. I hope it misses this phone booth. I don't want to be run over. I have too much to live for!"

"It's a good thing we write our feelings so we can read them, but I had to hear your voice too. And I wanted to tell you I won six awards in the Wisconsin Press Women's competition. I'll try to call you later if I can create some free minutes at home after work. I'm afraid of what I might say at work or at home. I love you so much.

And I can feel myself in you, too."

"I'm sending you another note. You should get it soon. I can't wait to see you again, hopefully without the construction noise and without talking from my little closet, unless you were here in it with me."

> We're not stars. Stars just sit there twinkling smugly.
> We're comets who sail through the jet-black sky of life
> Leaving trails of VIBRANT Energy Glowingly Alive!
> Making Once-in-a-Lifetime Experiences for the Spectators!

> In the past, I walked around in a blue fog.
> Today I am walking around in the most
> Incredible! Torrid! Red! Fog! Remembering.
> And remembering sets me Aflame!

> I am like a chambered nautilus.
> I have so many levels, so many chambers
> to get to the core, the base, the center of me.
> You take the route, round and round,
> down and down, breaking barriers.
> You did it today with courage
> and perseverance, patience and love.
> You found me at the core of my being
> where I was afraid I was lost
> and no one would ever reach again.
> Now I am open—One—Unity—Whole.
> Barriers broken down at last.
> A chambered nautilus no longer segmented.
> Open to the Sea of Love.

Jan on April 27, 1974

My heart is so filled with overwhelming joy in the beauty of it all. I went to work this morning and people, friends and acquaintances asked about the sparkle in my eyes. They'd answer their own question, "How are you?" with an immediate, "Marvelous.

Wonderful. I know. I know." And I would hold out my arms to symbolically embrace the world.

Today at work, Pat asked me what makes me so happy, and I paused, trying to think of the hundreds of reasons focused on one huge sweep of surging power. I love and am loved. I'm accepted and I'm accepting. I am a star shining with my other star, my Gemini. The pause was long before I returned my thoughts to her reality, and I answered that my Auxiliary slide production shown at their luncheon was warmly received, and more and more, and it was a beautiful day, and on and on.

She said she had a stomach ache. Later when I saw her as I was leaving, I said, "Have a good weekend, Pat. She nodded, "I know you'll have one."

I said, "Take good care of yourself.'

She looked at me and asked, "How?"

Phone booths are drawing me to them because I know when I use one to call, I'll have the tender and/or torrid response from the other end of the line. It never fails.

I had to call her today because I was afraid that when I'd see her tonight at Anne's, I'm apt to leap over the teeming mass of folk dancers and assorted characters, grab her and toss her to the couch— Hummm. What a thought!

At yesterday's conscious-raising session, we were asked how we felt about love and our past experiences with love. We both were so heady we could barely contain ourselves. We were sorry for those women who had nothing or only negative experiences with love. We had to be careful not to spill out our joy at what we've discovered, especially when the next question asked was, "Do you feel as though you can love another woman?" Our affirmations had to be subtle, of course, and we generated lots of laughs comparing the psychological or the physical aspects of "Can you love yourself?" For the question on "How much of your life is organized around love?" we both were prepared with a few poems so we could control our obsession. We wisely omitted the ecstatically blissful compositions that we'd written for each other.

Bea and I spent the rest of the day together before going home to our families.

Our yard work can wait. The winter's dead leaves can blow away. I've done enough of what I have to do. I have to pursue what I want to do. I asked myself once, "How can I get the response that I need?" I got it! It's real! I've felt the earth move.

Jan on Sunday, April 28, 1974

This afternoon, Alex entertained the next-door neighbor's young adult son and pal to sample his homemade wine in our living room while I worked at the family room table out of their sight. Their male voices faded while I semi-consciously absorbed TV scenes from the old movie classic, *Blood and Sand.* Rita Hayworth had seduced Bullfighter Tyrone Power away from his true and blameless fiancé, Linda Darnell. Rita reduced him to a weak, worshipful lover. Despite his tight toreador pants, Tyrone knelt in front of Rita, her white satin gown shimmering, her dark hair flowing down her shoulders. She had won. Without a sword, she made him kneel. Flamenco guitar tempos throbbed with powerful strokes. I thought of my lover and her influence over me. We each could play either of those parts, and I shivered with the potential for more—at whatever the cost.

My erotic mood was broken with the memory of my first high school talent show performance when I had the adolescent courage to play at being Rita Hayworth's Gilda, a sexy woman of the world singing, "Put the Blame on Mame" while discarding elbow-length gloves. I even threw in a little of Lauren Bacall's "The Look." Ha! What did I know then?

The men's laughter broke into my daydreaming. Their topic was ecology and underutilization of methane gas—but cows don't crap fast enough."

Bea on April 28, 1974

Dear Rachael,

I have been thinking. (Hurrah! About time! Ole!) I said to some friends that TA and I let Jan out of the bottle. (TA and Jan let me out of my bottle.) As a technique, it tears out corks and releases inner essences.

How wonderful for you to be a cork popper. I hesitate to say corkscrew, yet why the Hell not? Screw—Human expression of total communication that it is—to let people out of bottles. There should be a game term for that. Your TA creator Eric Berne missed a bet. A corkscrew. Better than a cavalier. Rachael Sandler, Corkscrew! (How about that for your business card?)

I love you, Rachael! But then I love a lot of people and things. It doesn't matter that I do and yet it does because "love emphasizes strong feelings and deep attachments and is used to express the emotions of love." (*Thorndike-Barnhart Dictionary*) And loving people and things are my problems, but what wonderful problems to have. There is something wrong with the "I'm O.K. You're O.K." philosophy because it should be "I'm Terrific, You're Terrific!" The hell with O.K. That's only mediocre. And "loving" means to care a lot, which I do, and so do you!

At my stage of life, I have decided I may not be able to set the world on fire anymore, but if I can just char a little corner of it, I'll be happy. You char corners, keep charring. You're terrific!

Jan let me see the beautiful letter that you wrote her about her journal. Goddamn, I wished I had said all of it. Thank you for saying it so beautifully for all of us.

I hope you can accept Jan's invitation to our TA reunion dinner on May 4 because I've been invited too. I'm supposed to go to a symposium in Chicago on scuba diving that day, and I am, but if there is a chance to socialize with you.

Love,
Bea

Jan on April 29, 1974

Kent State happened on May 2, 1970, when four students are killed and eleven wounded. 2nd Lt. William Calley and his men massacred Vietnam civilians. Daniel Ellsberg stole the Pentagon papers; our UU Beacon Press published them. The Berrigan priest brothers are put in jail for destroying draft records.

On August 24, 1970, the fierce anger of Madison's protesters was defused by the bombing of UW's Sterling Hall that killed researcher Robert Fassnacht, a father of three children. The war and war protesting comes even closer to home.

My assignments took me to UW-Oshkosh where Jerry Rubin, a Yippie! and a member of the Chicago 7, targeted the United States, its war priorities and its values.

I reported, "Radical revolutionary Jerry Rubin used words like pellets from a loud shotgun blast which hits every space on the target including the background.

"Underground newspaper editor Mark Knops (who went to jail rather than reveal his sources for a story on the bombing of the University of Wisconsin Army Math Research center) zeroed within the target quietly saying, 'Sabotage is the answer to destroy the American empire."

It was a tricky business capturing the words of the agitators' fast-talking tirades while being unbiased as a reporter. Rubin blasted Nixon's losing control of the Army, officers being killed by their own men in Vietnam, consumer society, schools, and the anal personality, ecocide of the Vietnamese, racism, Christianity, Heaven, doctors and the profit motive, Spiro Agnew, Republican fascists, Democratic opportunists, Che Guevara, John Wayne, sick-male-ego syndrome, children's-, women's- and gay-rights liberations.

Mark Knops described the Madison campus as a grim, brooding Teutonic war-helmeted set of war-making buildings. "When you understand in your own head and see yourself as a rebellious serf inside your empire, you can choose to go on and help run that empire, or you can start to build a resistant culture to that empire, kill it, bring it down and liberate the entire planet...When you're in a corner, sabotage is the answer."

A noticeable lack of applause was obvious, and when student organizers passed the hat to pay for expenses, donations added up to only $110 dollars. Most of the four hundred curious students returned to their twelve-week exams and term papers.

A spectator of know the liar to embarrass Alex rather than mixing Rubin said, "Why did I ever come?"

Jan on April 29, 1974

I certainly don't get respect at home. Perhaps the notoriety of many of my stories embarrasses Alex rather than makes him proud. Perhaps he's jealous of my visibility. Perhaps it feeds his anger at my being a working mother—a highly visible one, too. And the more independent I become, the longer his steely gray hair and mustache grow.

Jan on April 30, 1974

On my April calendar and notes, I tallied remembrances of our making love seventeen times with advancing complexity. We had seven rendezvous, seven casual but intense meetings, and spent three whole days together. I was also satisfying my husband at our usual frequency. Somewhere in this orgasmic life, Bea and I made love in the morning, Alex and I made love in the night and I was so turned on I made love to myself within the twenty-four hours that I made love with each of them.

But who's counting?

Jan on May 8, 1974

As if I didn't have enough on my agenda, I hosted a TA reunion dinner party on Saturday. Though the Lindbergs and the Muraks took both cars to drive to Chicago and the Underwater World Show, Bea made it to my house and joined Rachael, Marge, Anna, and others for supper. She played her guitar and we laughed and talked until 2 a.m. Alex was sullen for days.

Today she whistled and I came. She wrote another song for me, "Mother Earth" and I cried at the beauty of it. I think it should be a universal anthem for our planet. I'll send Judy Collins a copy.

MOTHER EARTH

> Mother Earth, Mother Earth.
> Nurture me for I love thee.
> Lake and hill, can't get my fill

of your sweet land, your sea and sand,
your trees and sky,
 your mountains high.
I love them all, your spring and fall,
your warmth and snow.
All these I know are mine,
my Mother Earth.

Mother Earth, Mother Earth.
I in turn will nurture thee
to keep you free for all
to see for all to share preserve with care,
my precious Mother Earth.
My precious Mother Earth.
My precious Mother Earth.

Bea on May 10, 1974

I'm playing my/your song for everybody. In essence, I'm shouting from the rooftops where I only danced before. Response? Doug, the lead guitar in a band, my kids' friend, and my guitar teacher, said, "It's beautiful. Mother Earth, Eh? It's not like anything else."

I sing it with the most incredible secret joy— "My precious Mother Earth…" The rest of these guys, I think, think it is corny, and it is, sort of on the surface, but at its real meaning level. Well, we know—My precious Mother Earth.

THE END

UPCOMING BOOKS
From Mother Courage Press

Additional Books in the Eight-Book
Whistling Girls & Crowing Hens Series

Book 2—*Gullibles' Travels,* where divorced Bea tries not to be a lesbian and her lover Jan strives to keep her children, husband and Bea happy. Bea and friends test the Sexual Revolution of the '60s and '70s. Jan recalls living in Cold War Germany in the '50s and touring Greece, Leningrad, and Moscow with her husband in the '70s. Jan defuses a labor/management conflict and Bea and Jan escape to Europe for a rowdy and risqué three-week escapade in '76.

Book 3—*In Secret Transgressions*, Jan's hospital PR job expands with Bea as her assistant. Jan's marriage turns raw. Divorce. Bea submits to sexual harassment in the workplace, is fired, and Jan is emotionally harassed on the job. Travel helps them heal and they create Mother Courage Bookstore and Press.

Book 4—*Being Mother Courage* (1976-89) embodies a dream come true: creating a feminist bookstore and experiencing historic events and adventures in the women's movement and the gay/lesbian world. They attended their first American Booksellers Association (ABA) trade show in Los Angeles, and ending by sailing with Seaworthy Women on a 31-foot wooden ketch launched from the 5000-boat Marina del Rey to Catalina Island. Women's spirituality circles and lesbian support groups in Bea and Jan's home inspire and support women. Jan confronts job harassment and Bea faces the bookstore's demise. Their Cancun vacation fun ignores sun-bathing on beaches to explore Mayan ruins. Jan enters the snorkeling world led by scuba-diver Bea. At home, their full moon circles begin with feminist and original rites and rituals. Tension turns to courageous laughter when conflicts are overcome. Bea uses her skills to pioneer Apple's Mac desktop publishing and was a guest speaker/teacher at the International Women's Booksellers Conference in Spain.

For additional information on the series, contact:
Editor and Publisher Jeanne Arnold
MotherCouragePress31@gmail.com

ABOUT JAN ANTHONY

I'm not shy, but I'm not rowdy. I'm a feminist but I'm not strident. I'm from a small city but I've been around. I lived a straight life for half of it and I chose to live a lesbian life with my lover for the other half. I'm a relentless optimist, a friend, mother, grandmother and great-grandmother. And we all love each other.

I write these stories for you from decades of living. Some are sad or angry but most are happy and rowdy and, when appropriate, I'll slip in some of my free-thinking values. My t-shirt says, "Sweet old lady? More like battle-tested warrior queen."

Mother Courage Press
MotherCouragePress31@gmail.com

www.ingramcontent.com/pod-product-compliance
Lightning Source LLC
LaVergne TN
LVHW021811060526
838201LV00058B/3326